🦴 DELHI HAS 325,000 STREET DOGS

DEDICATED TO OUR MUTT, BUTTERCUP

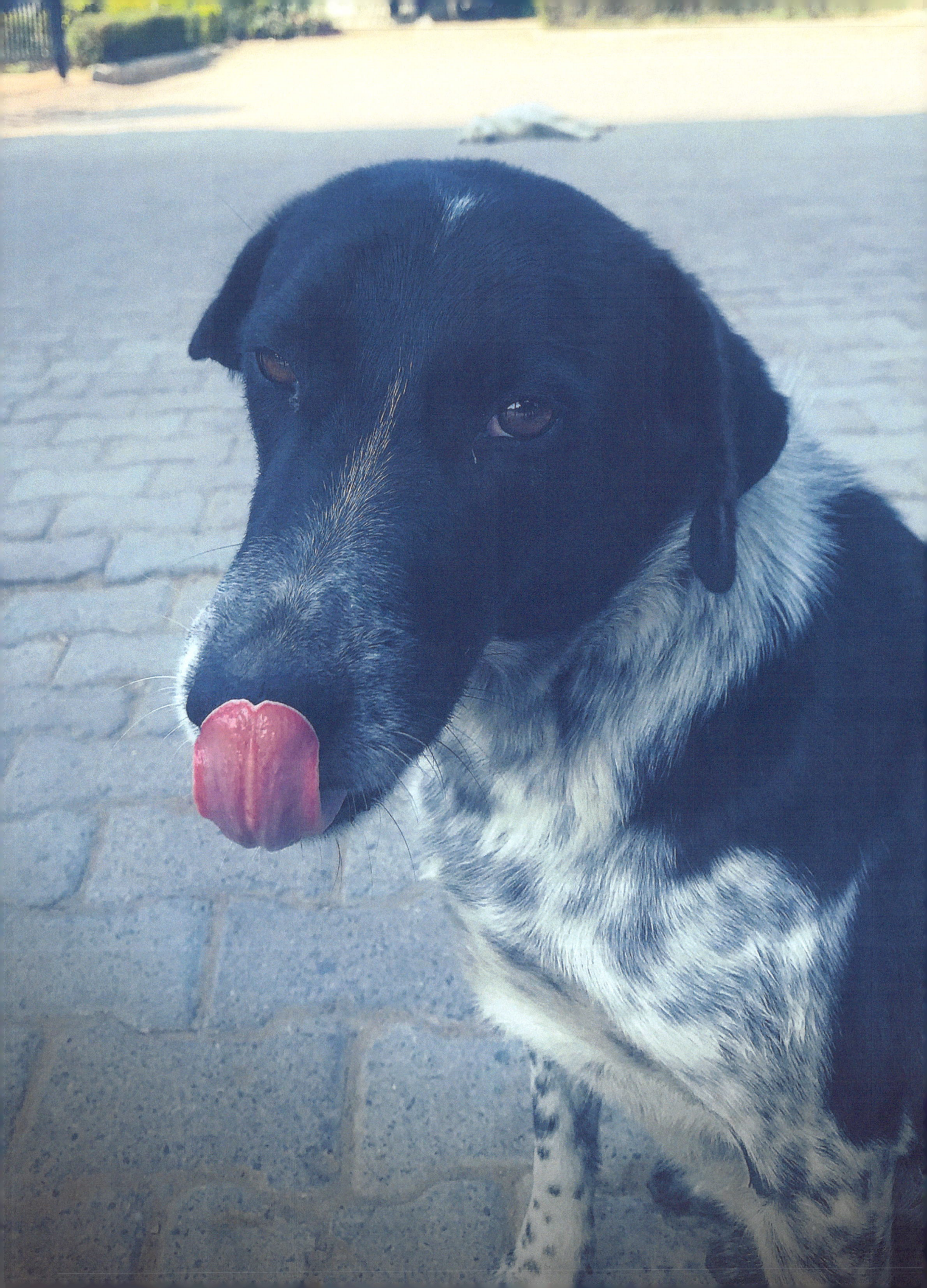

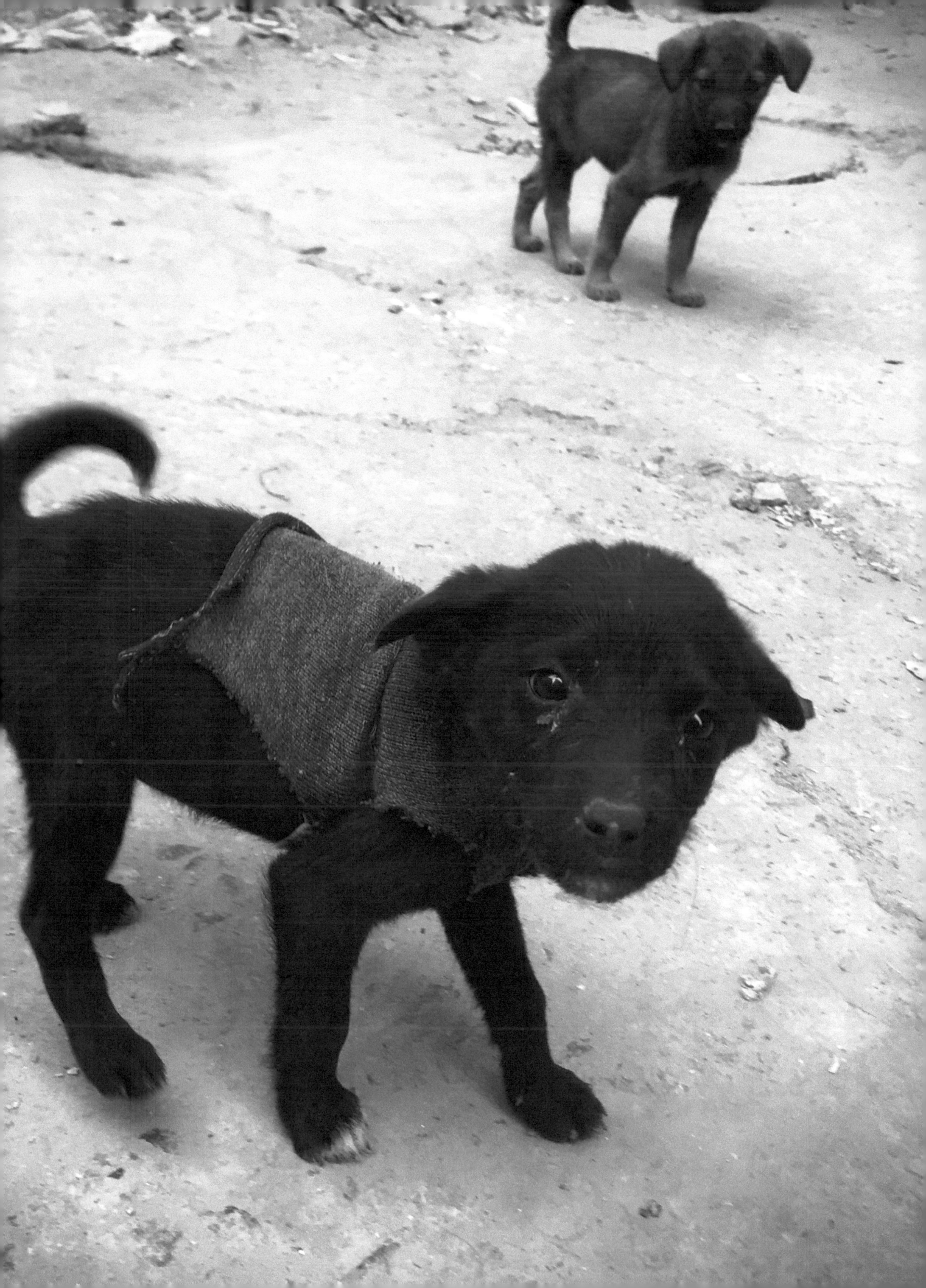

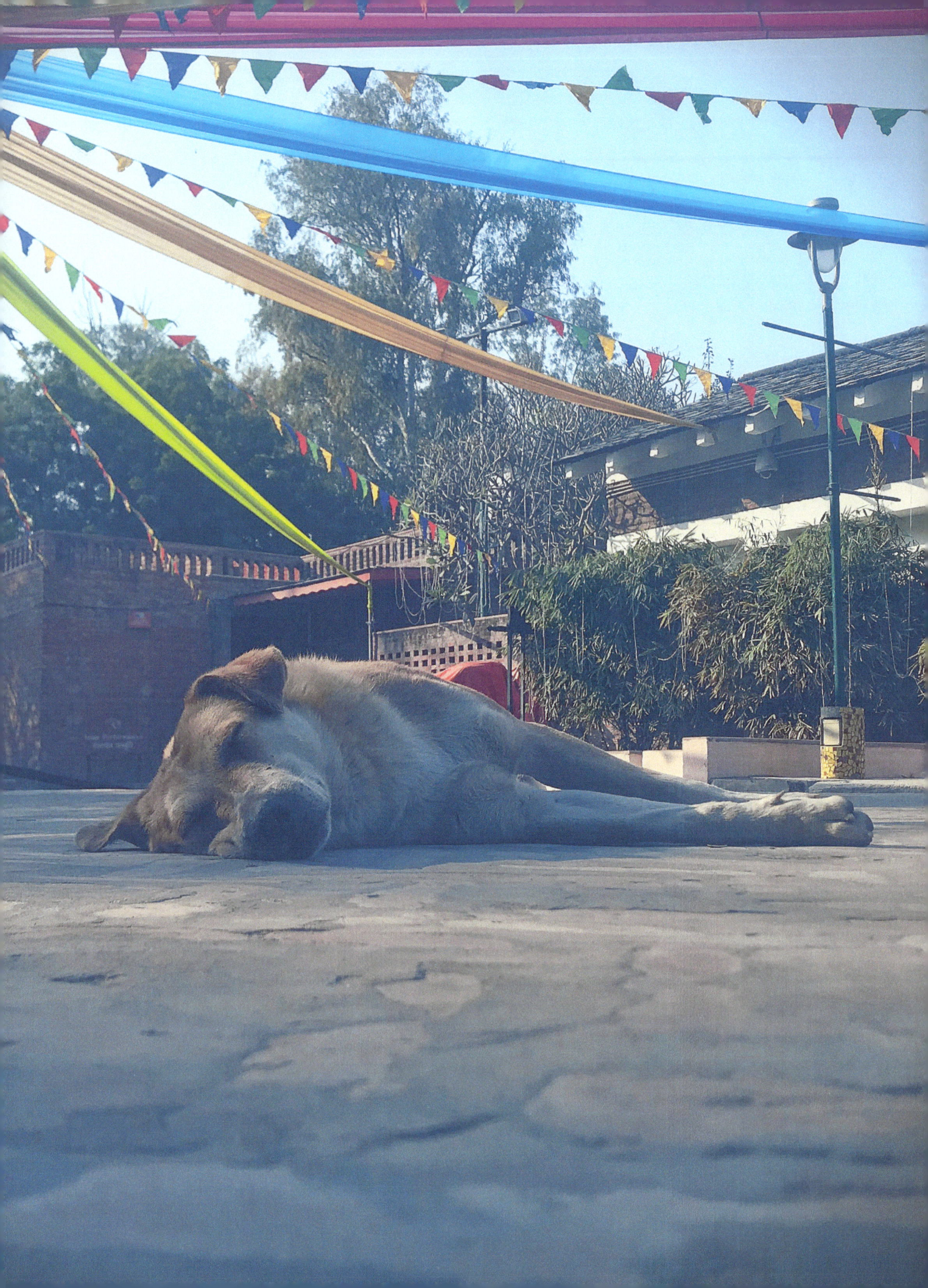

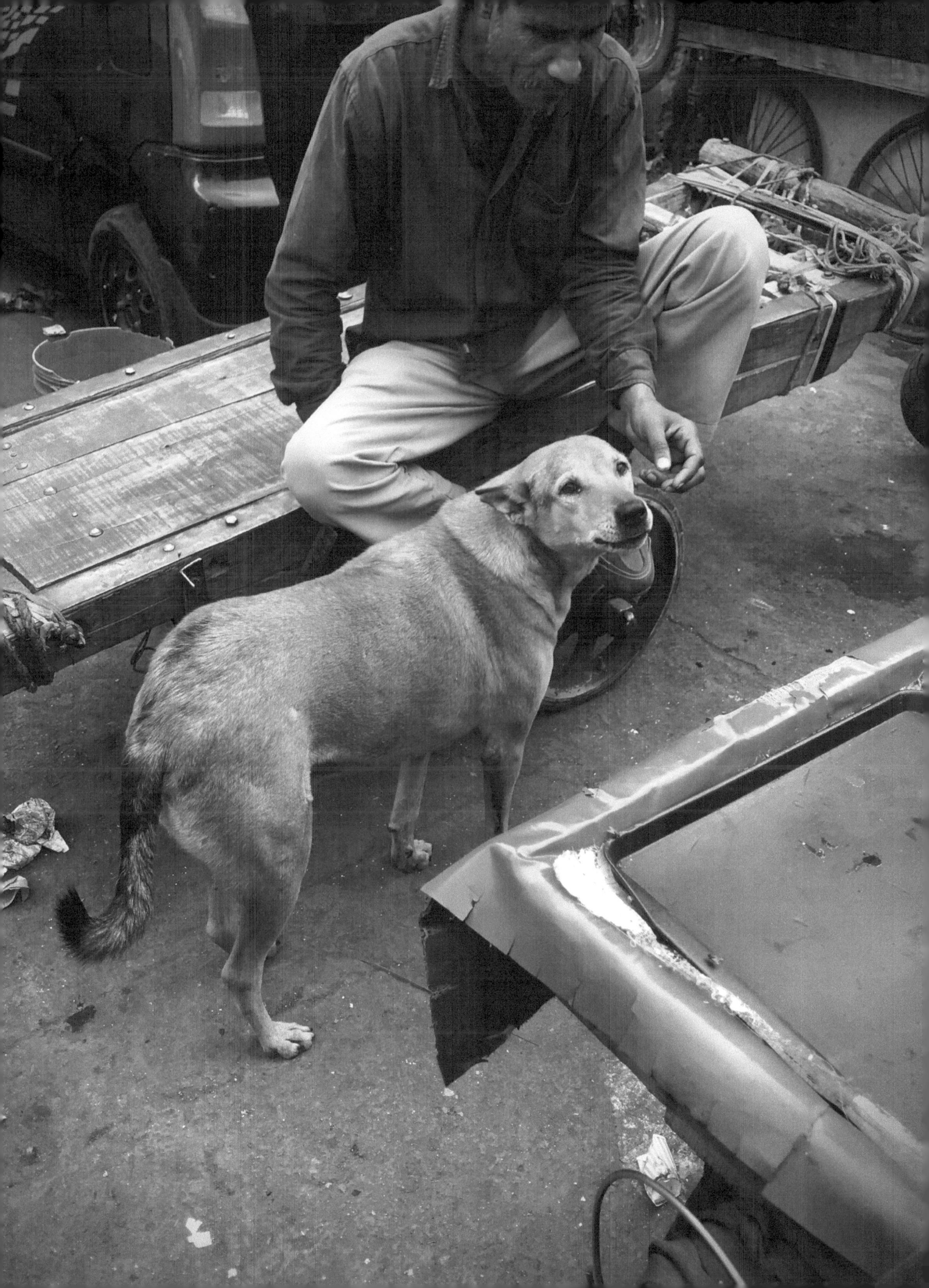

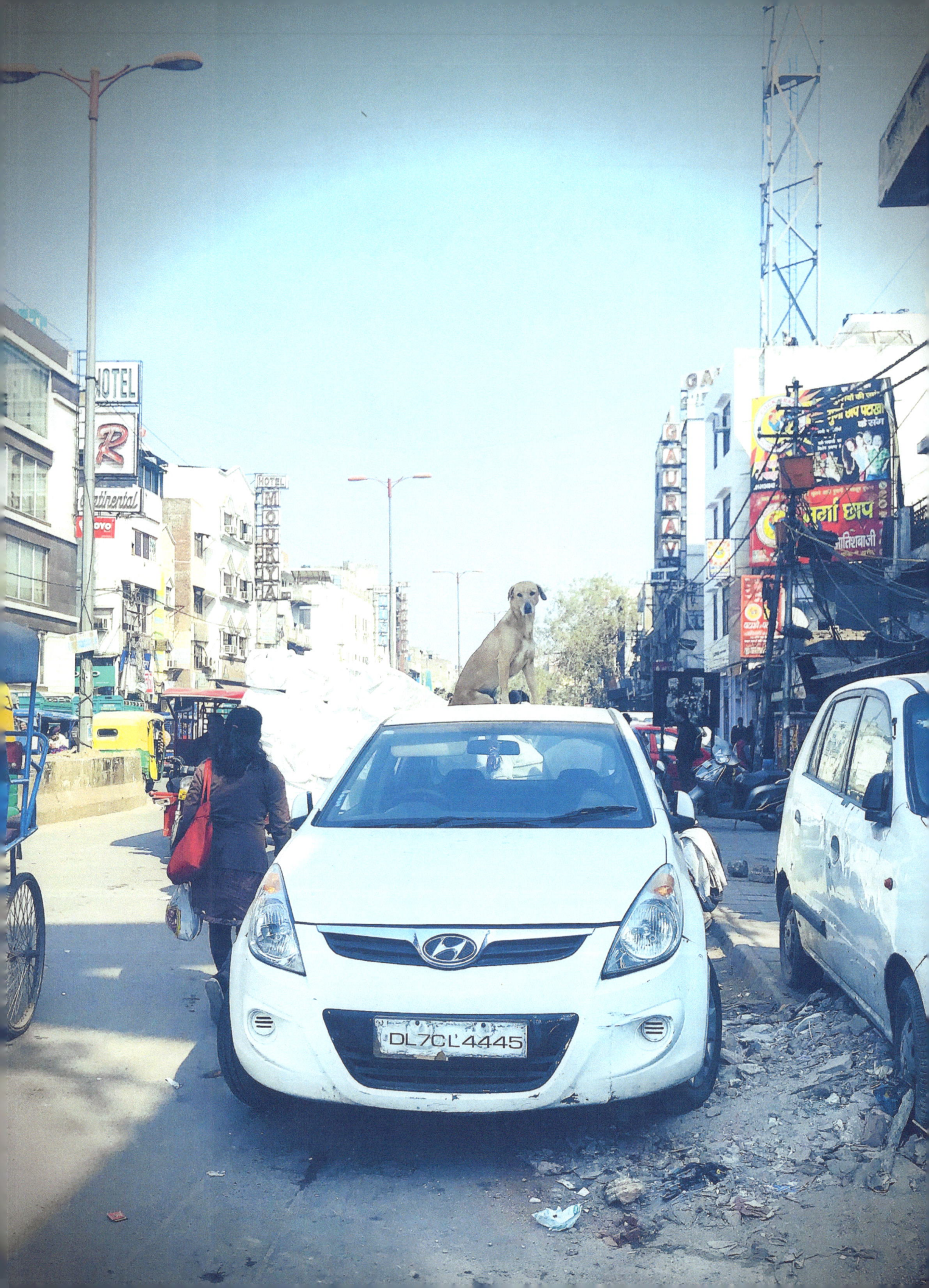

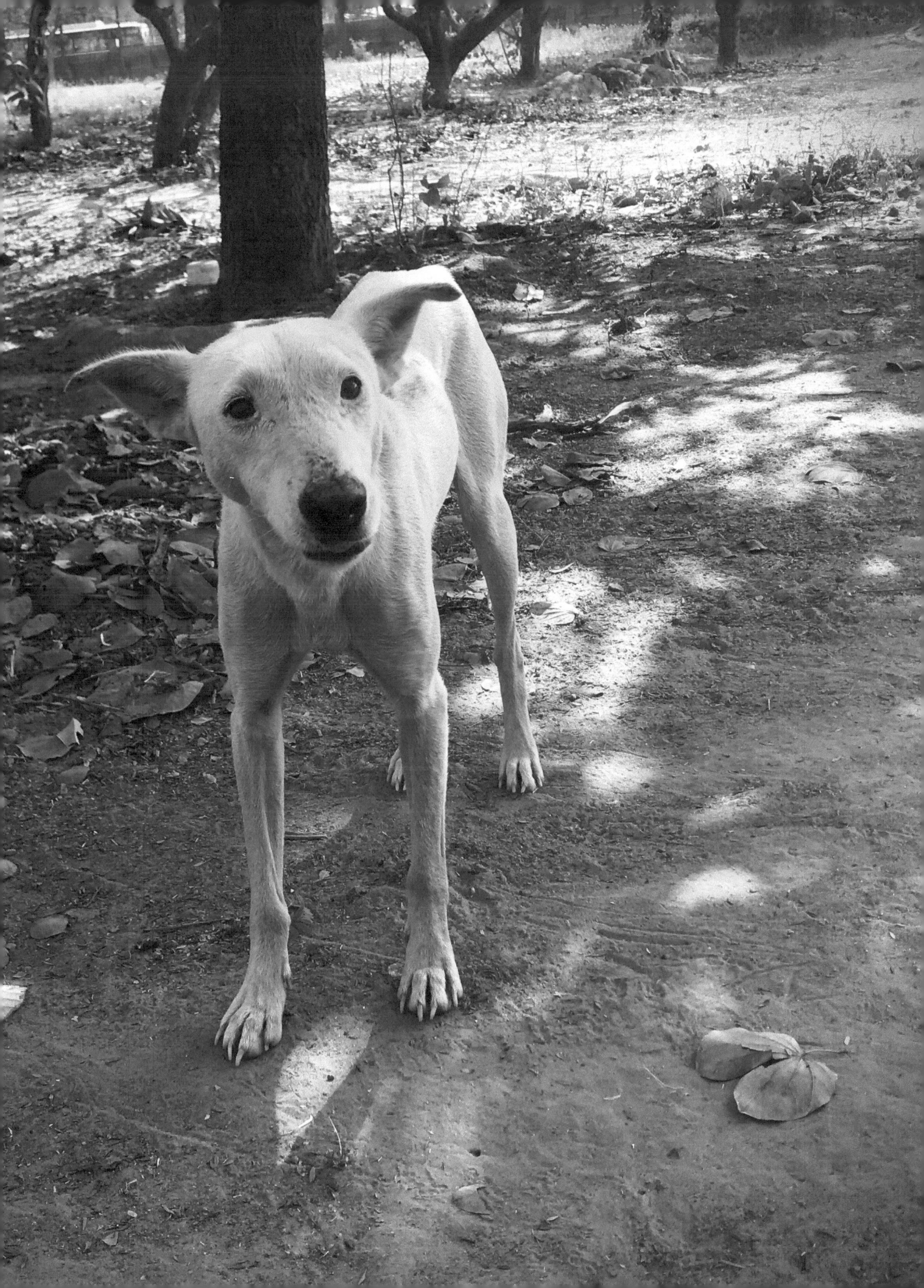

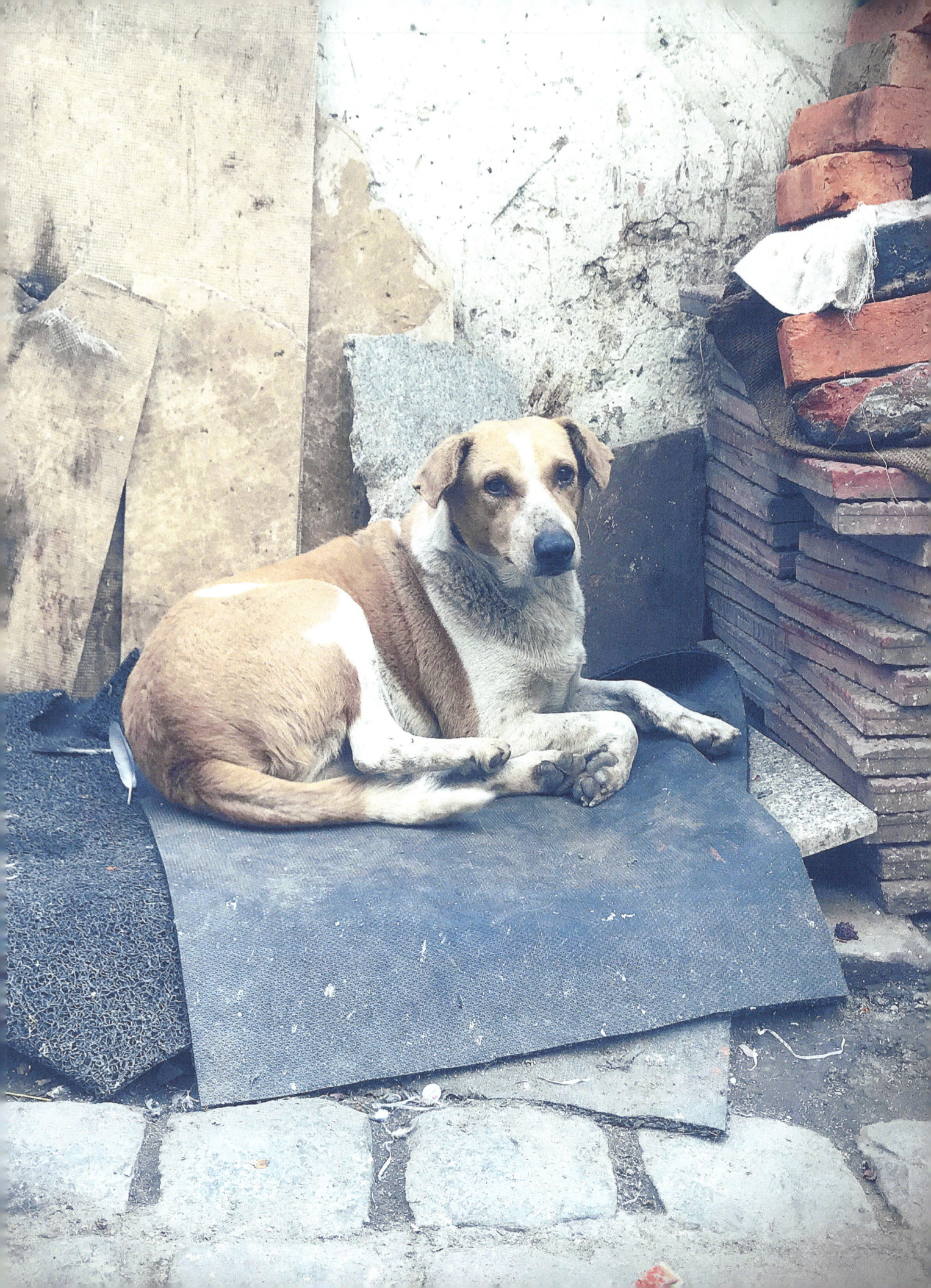

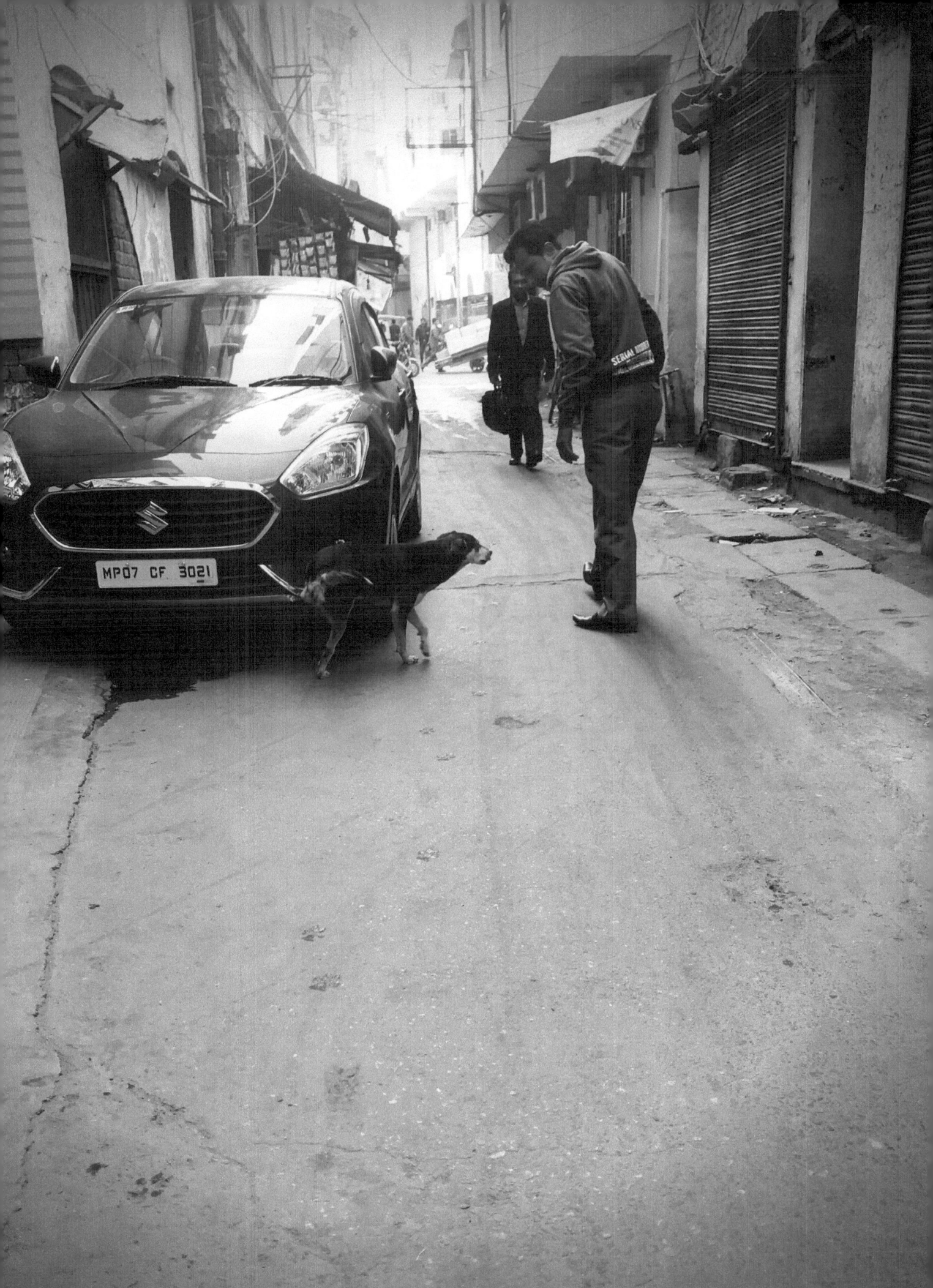

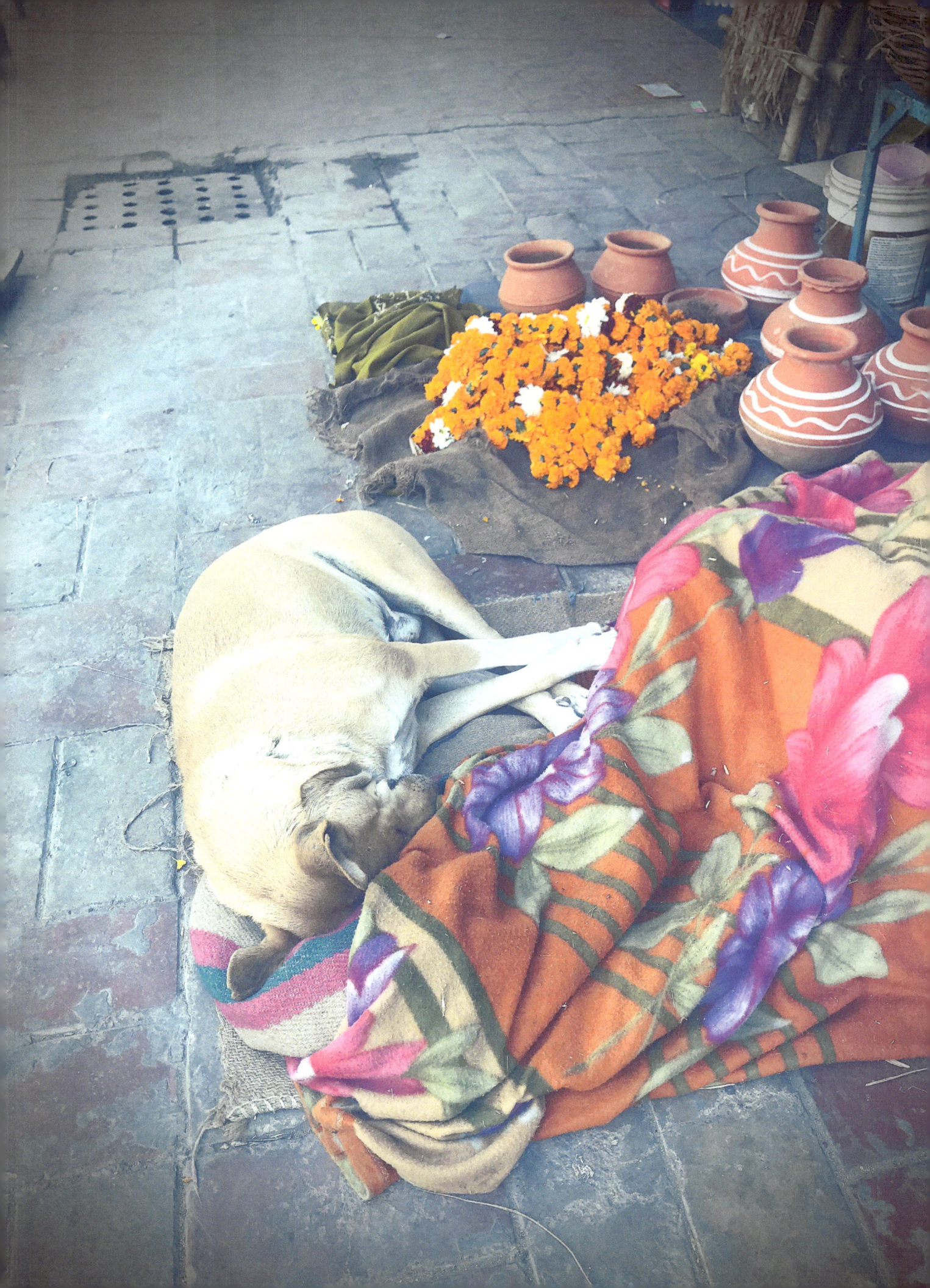

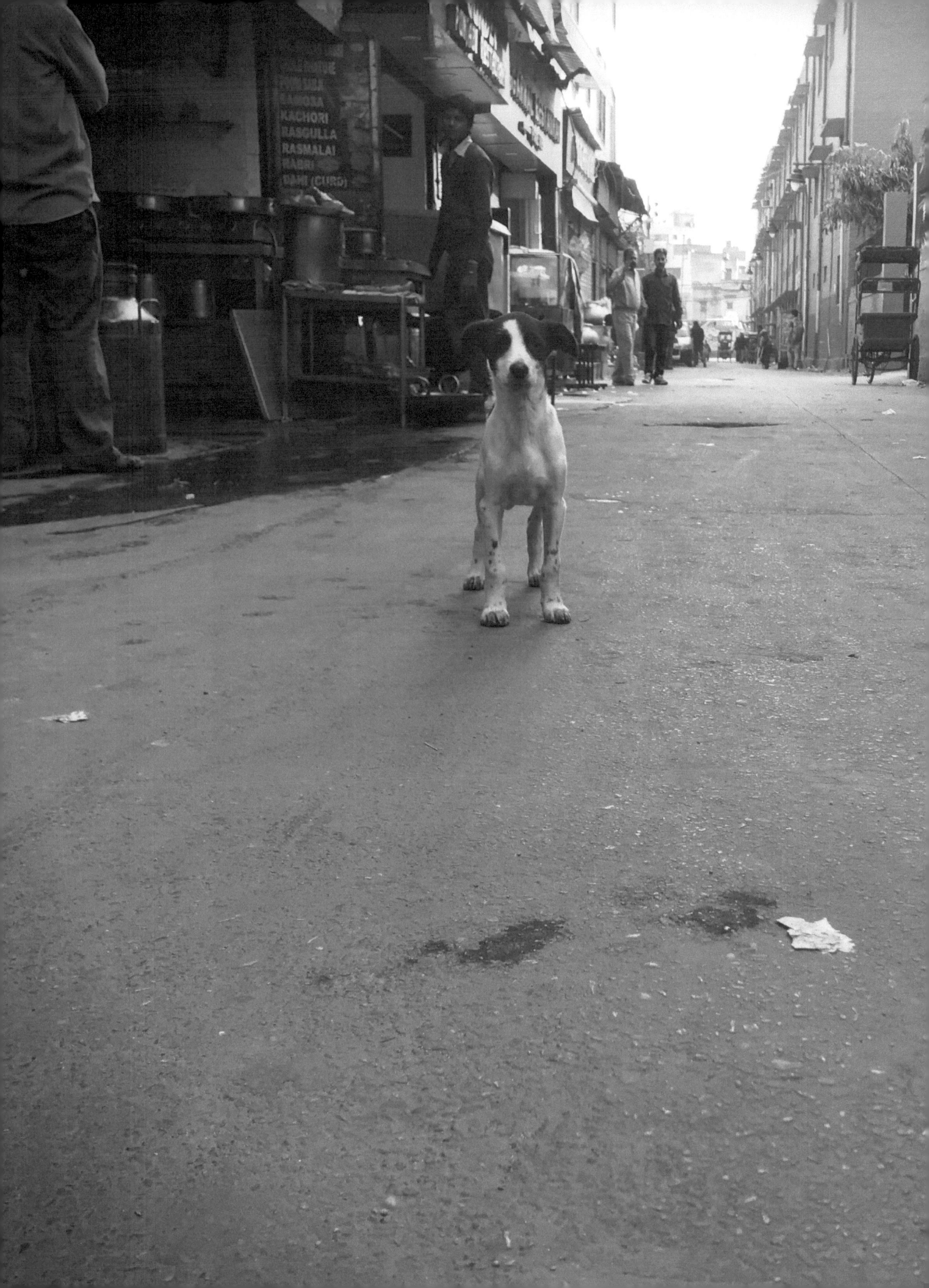

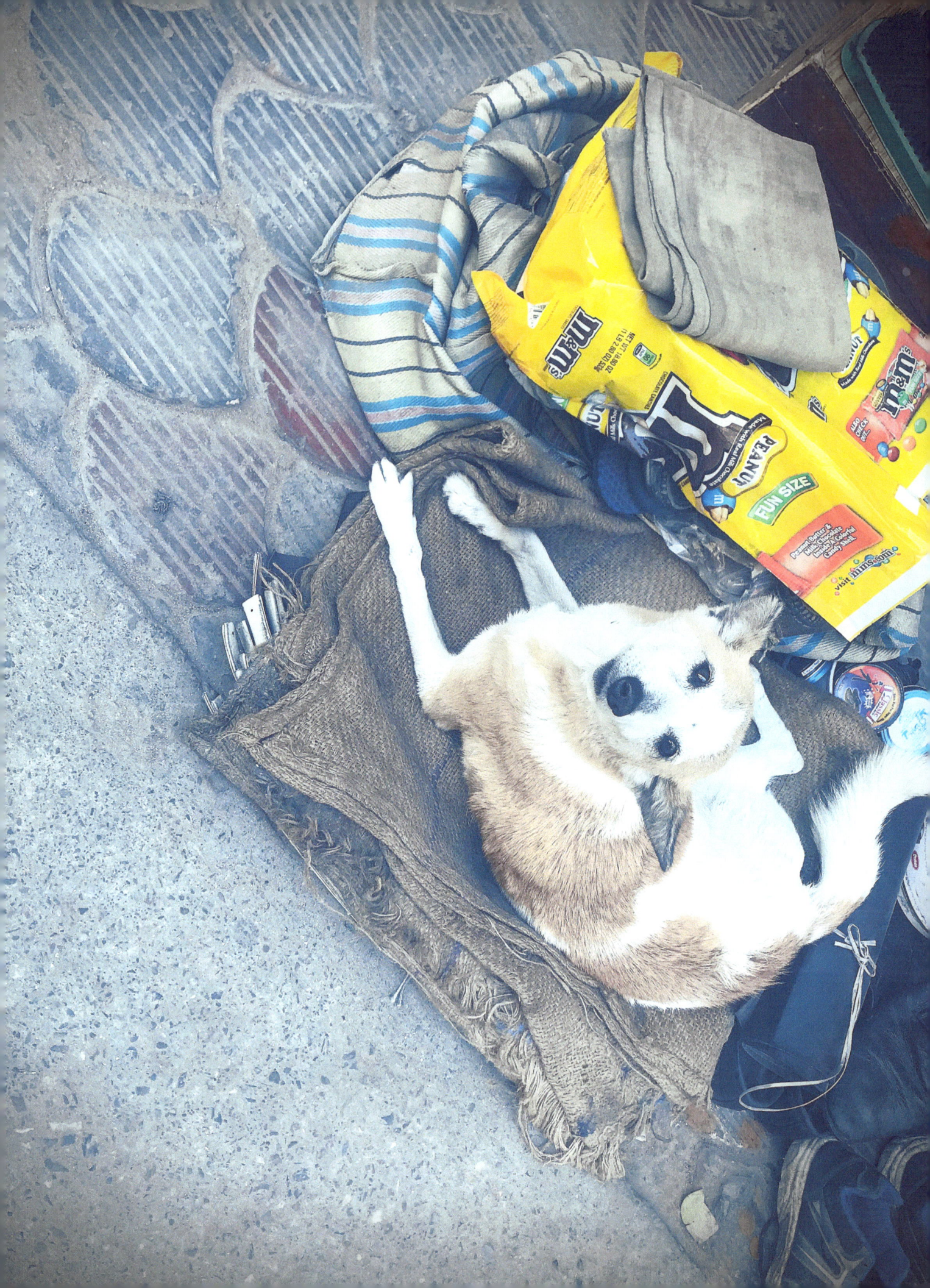

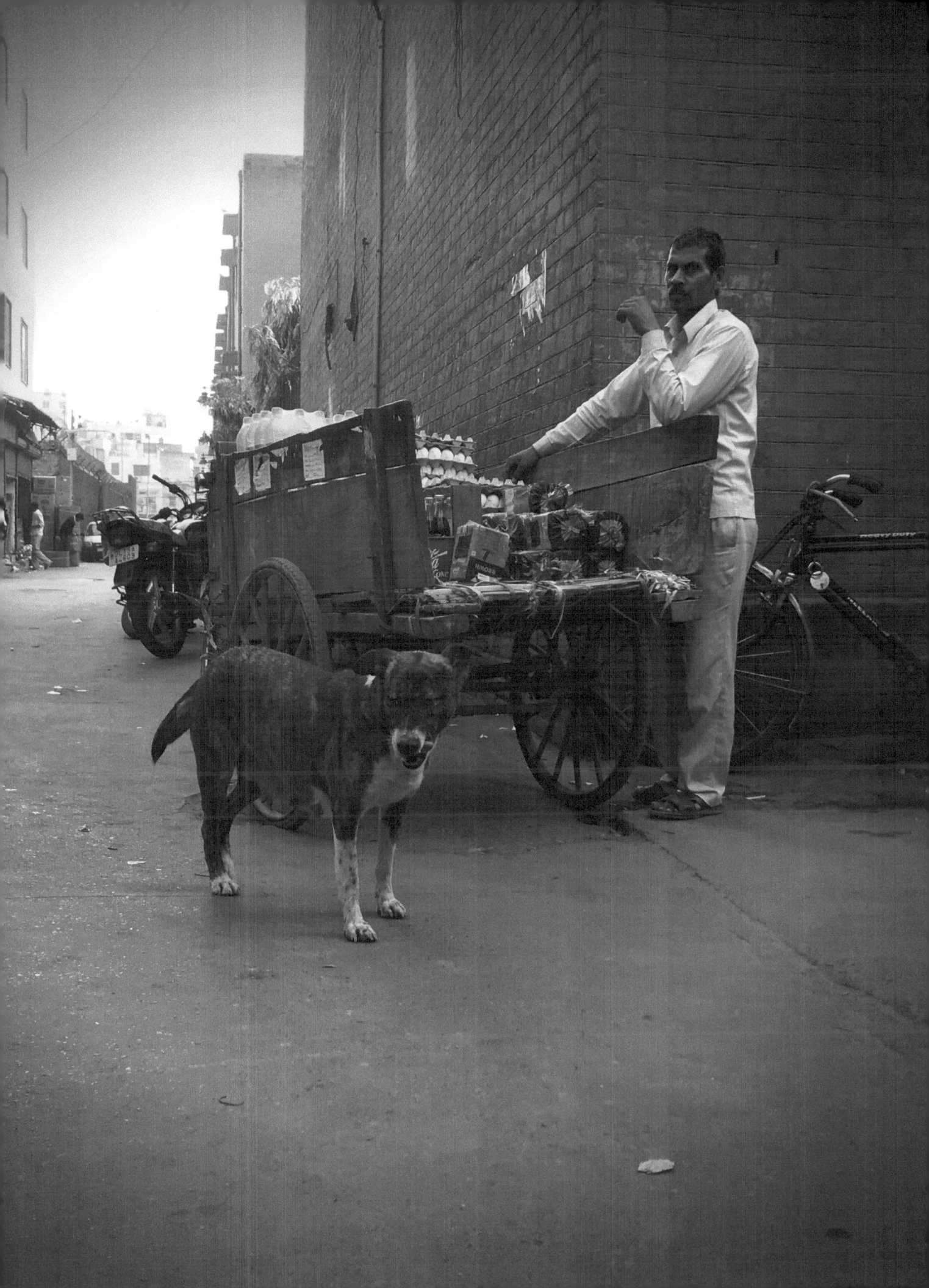

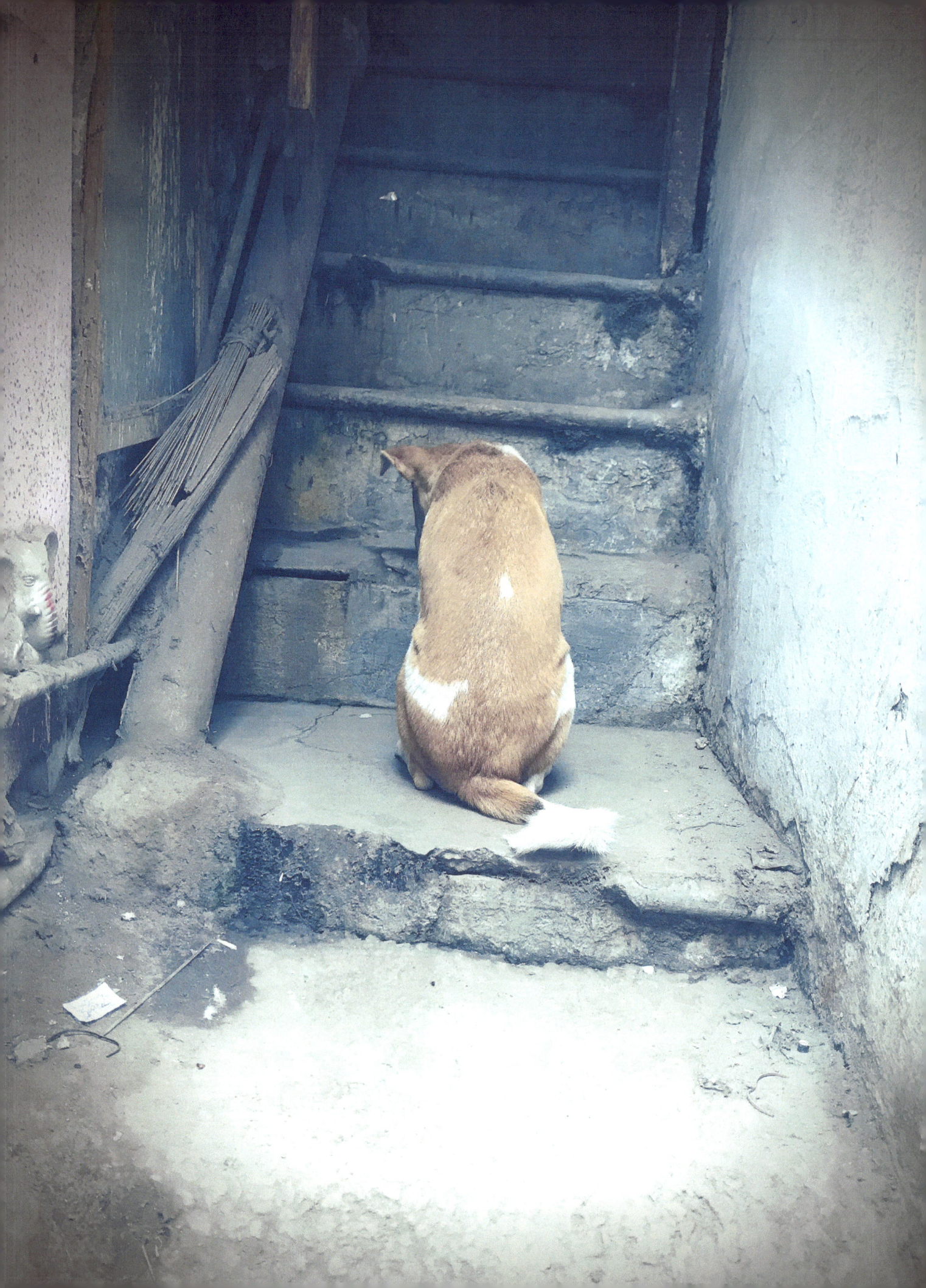

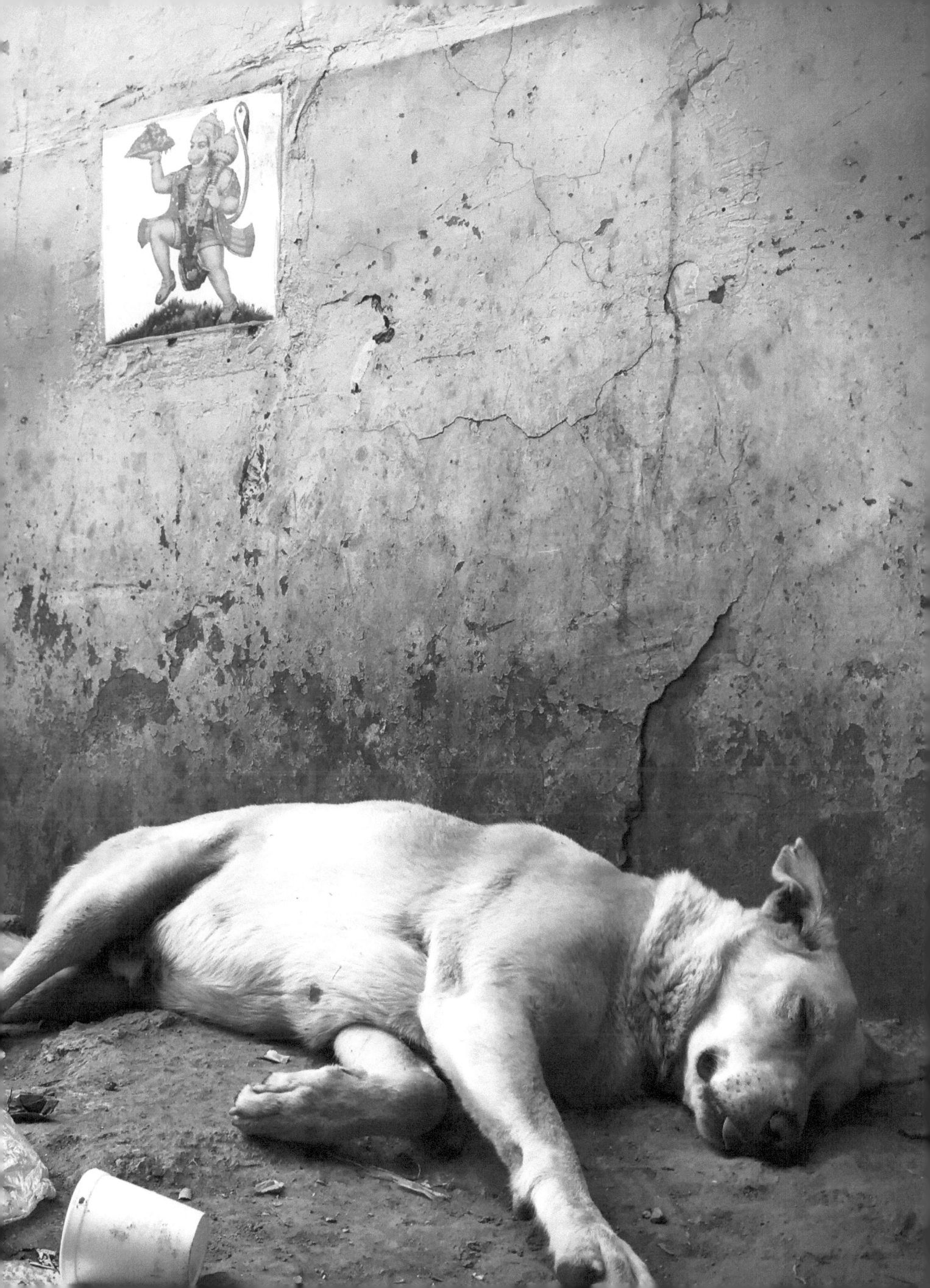

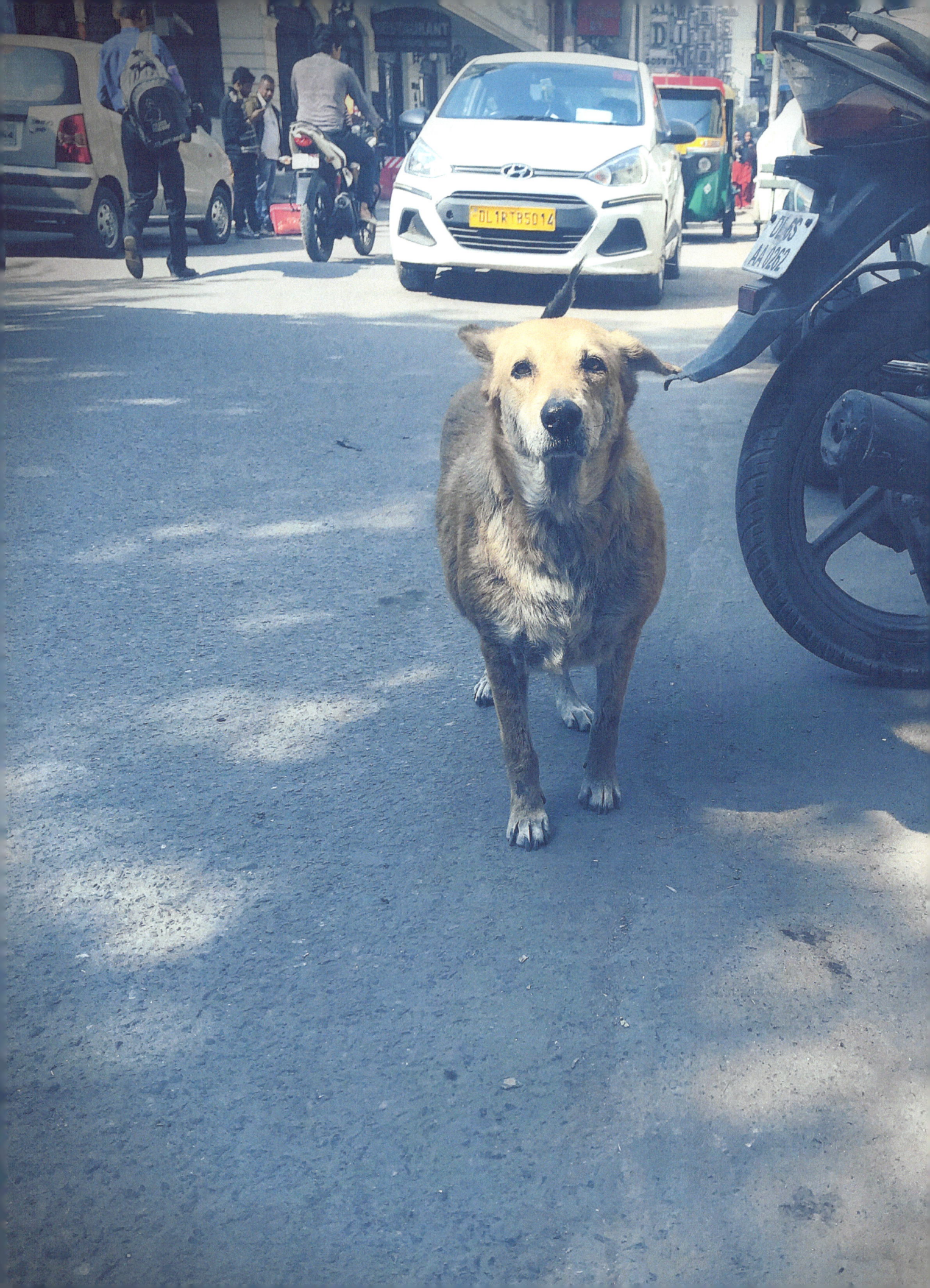

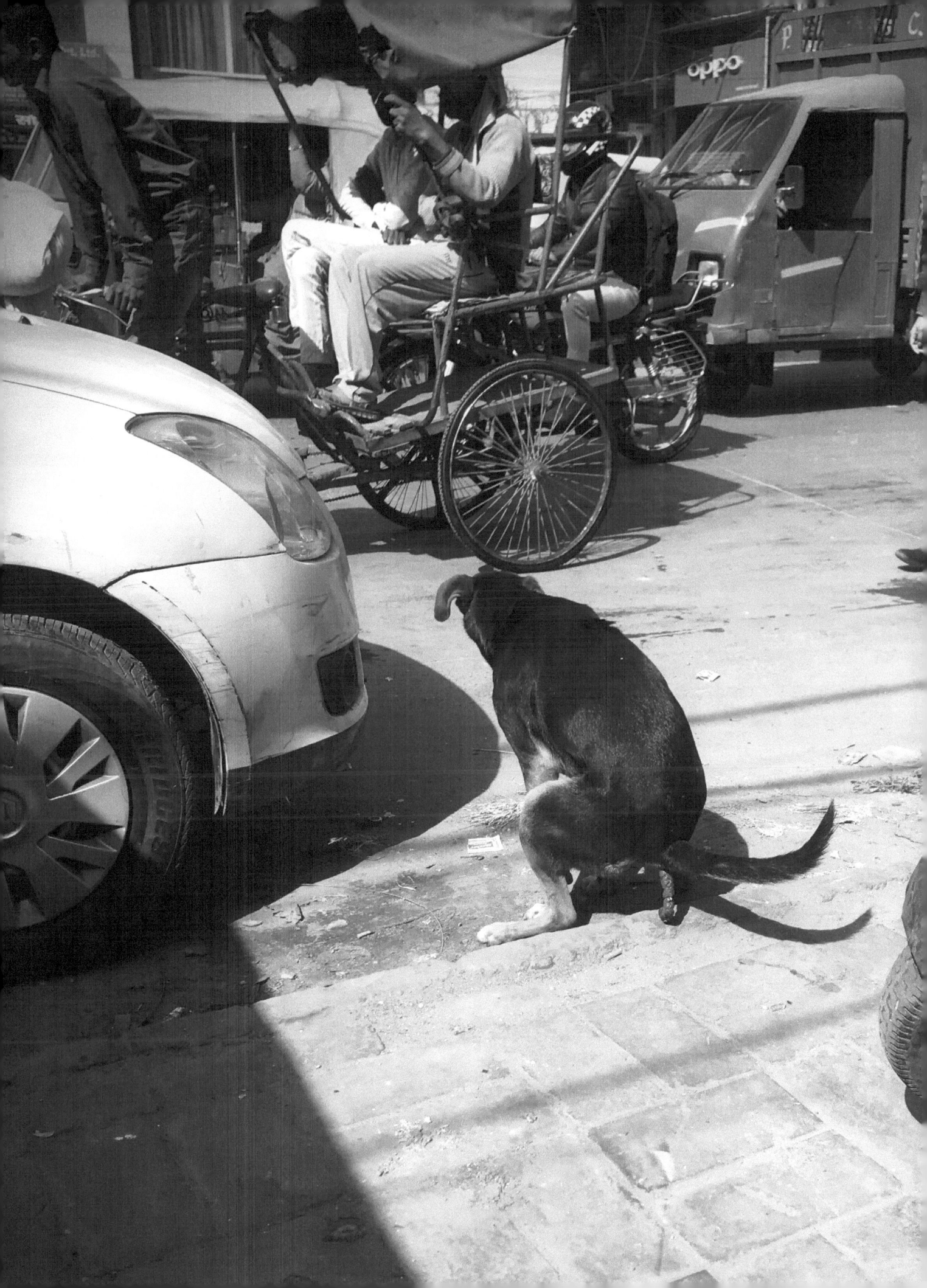

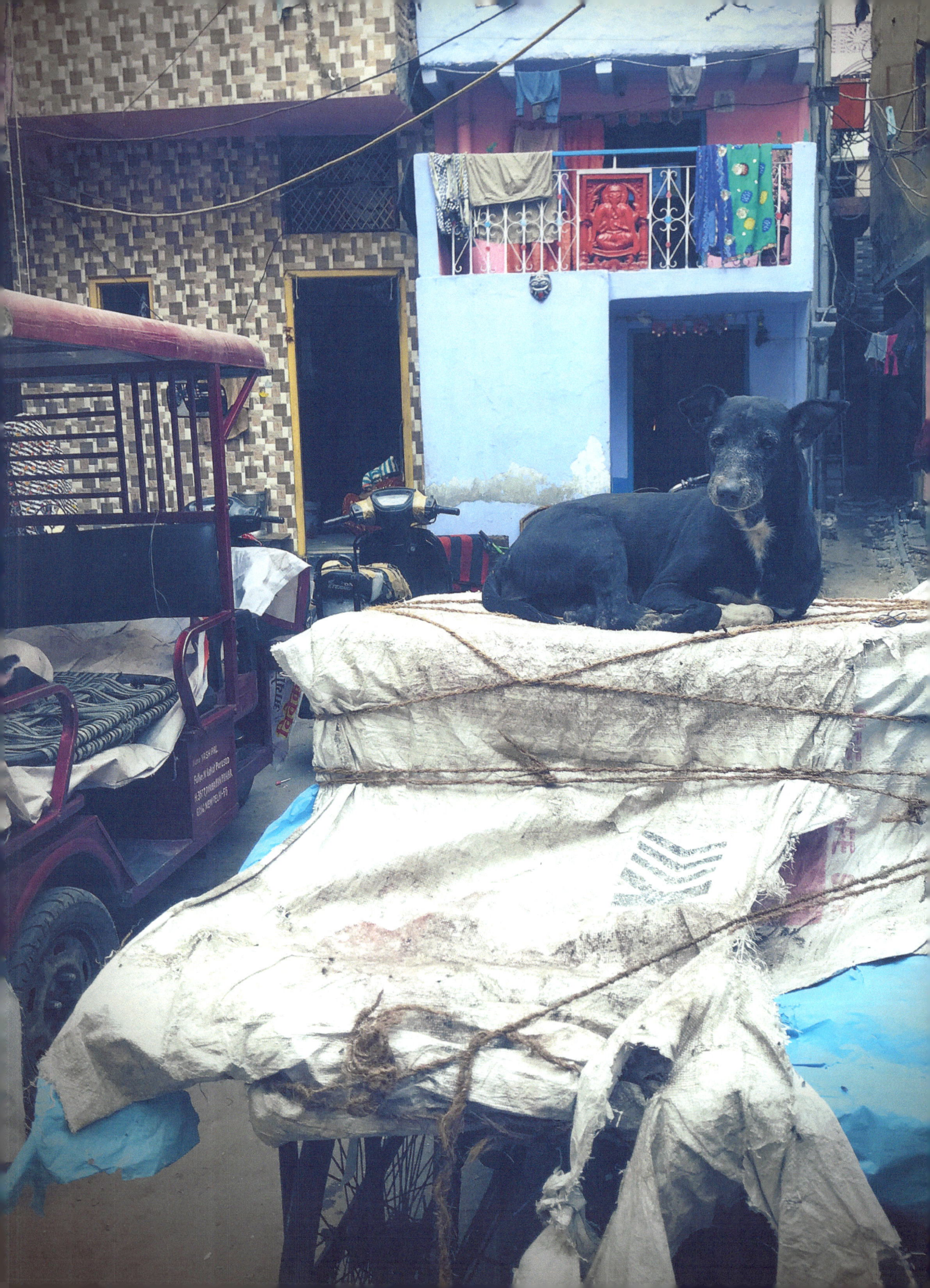

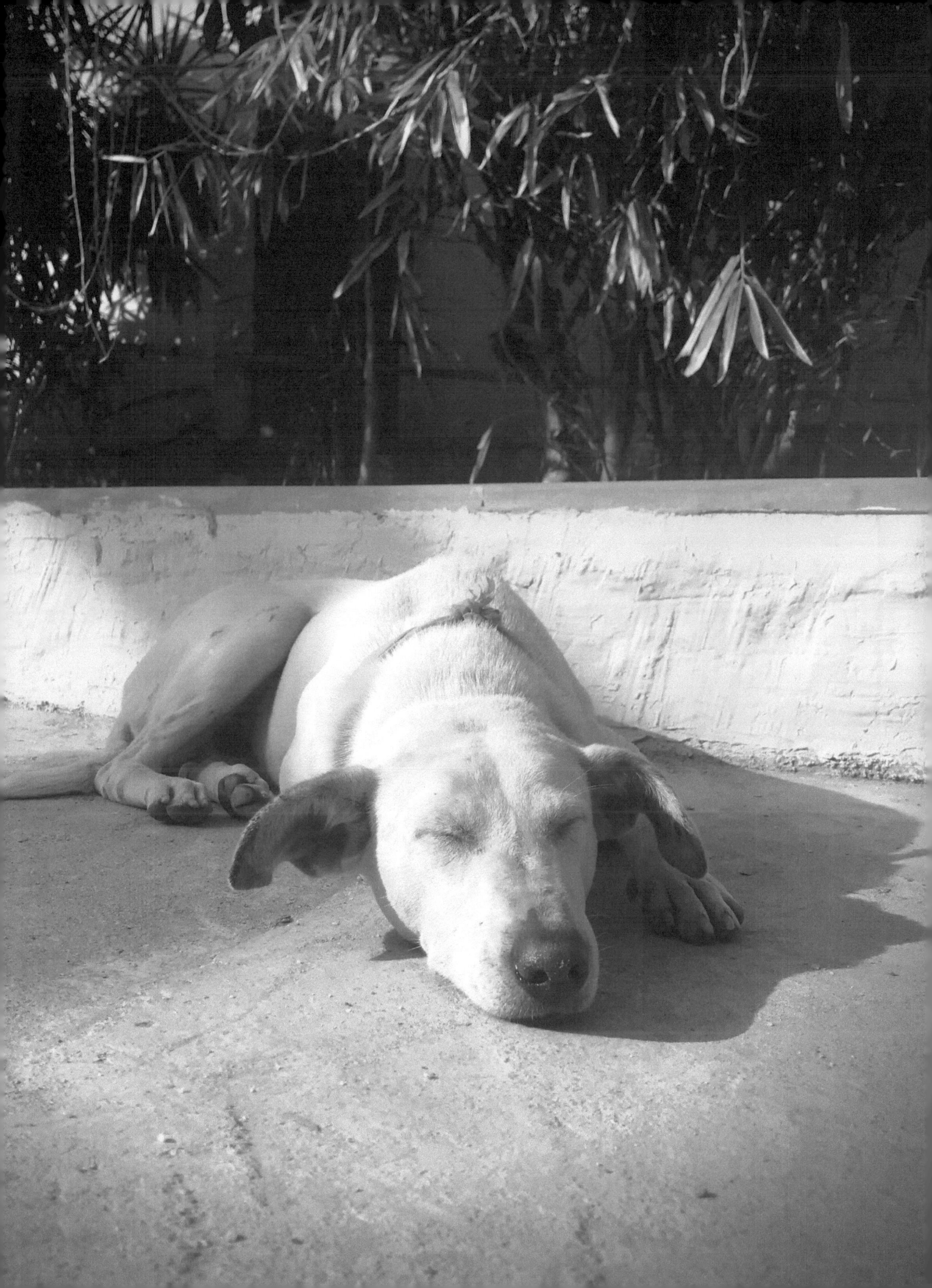

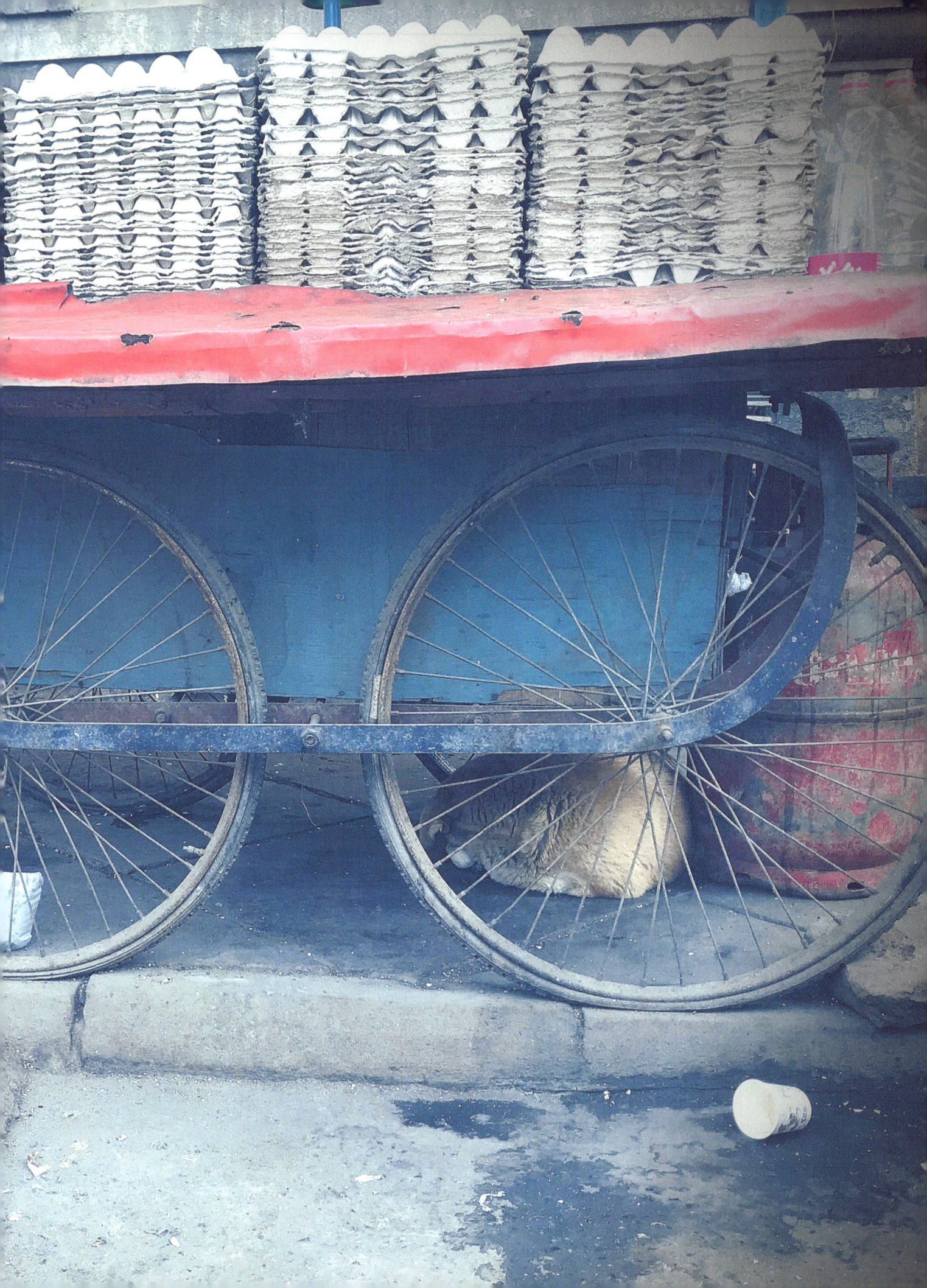

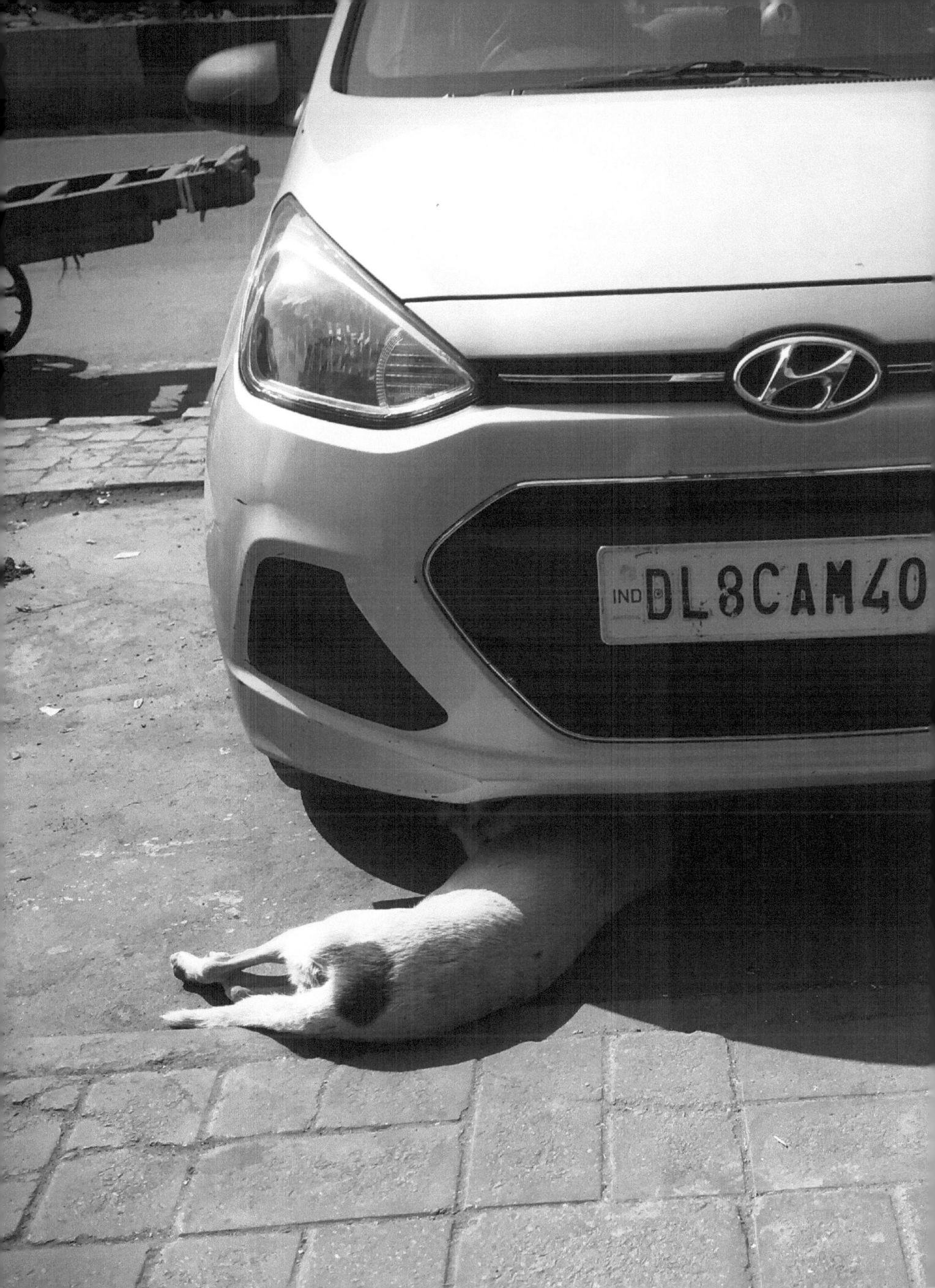

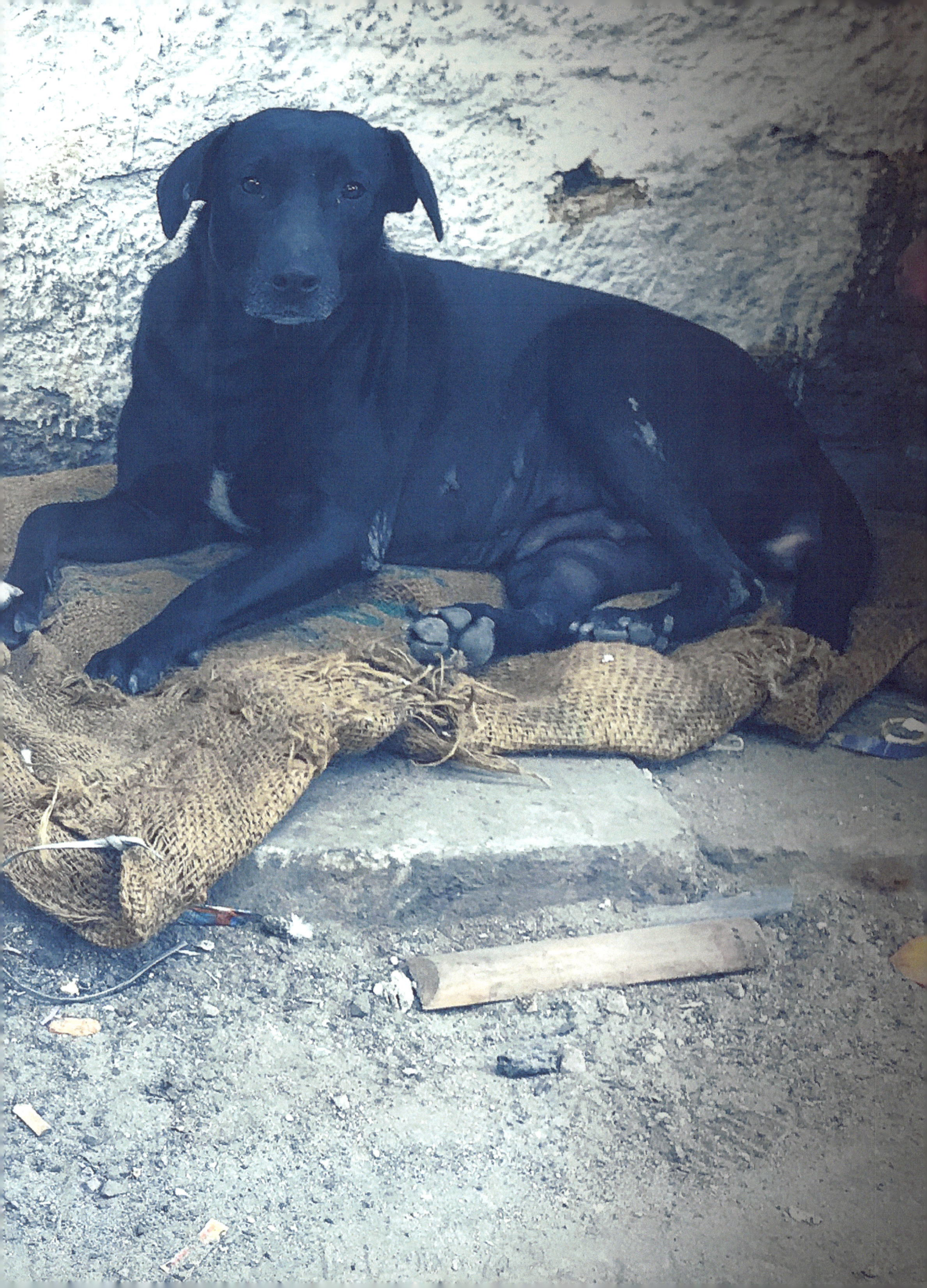

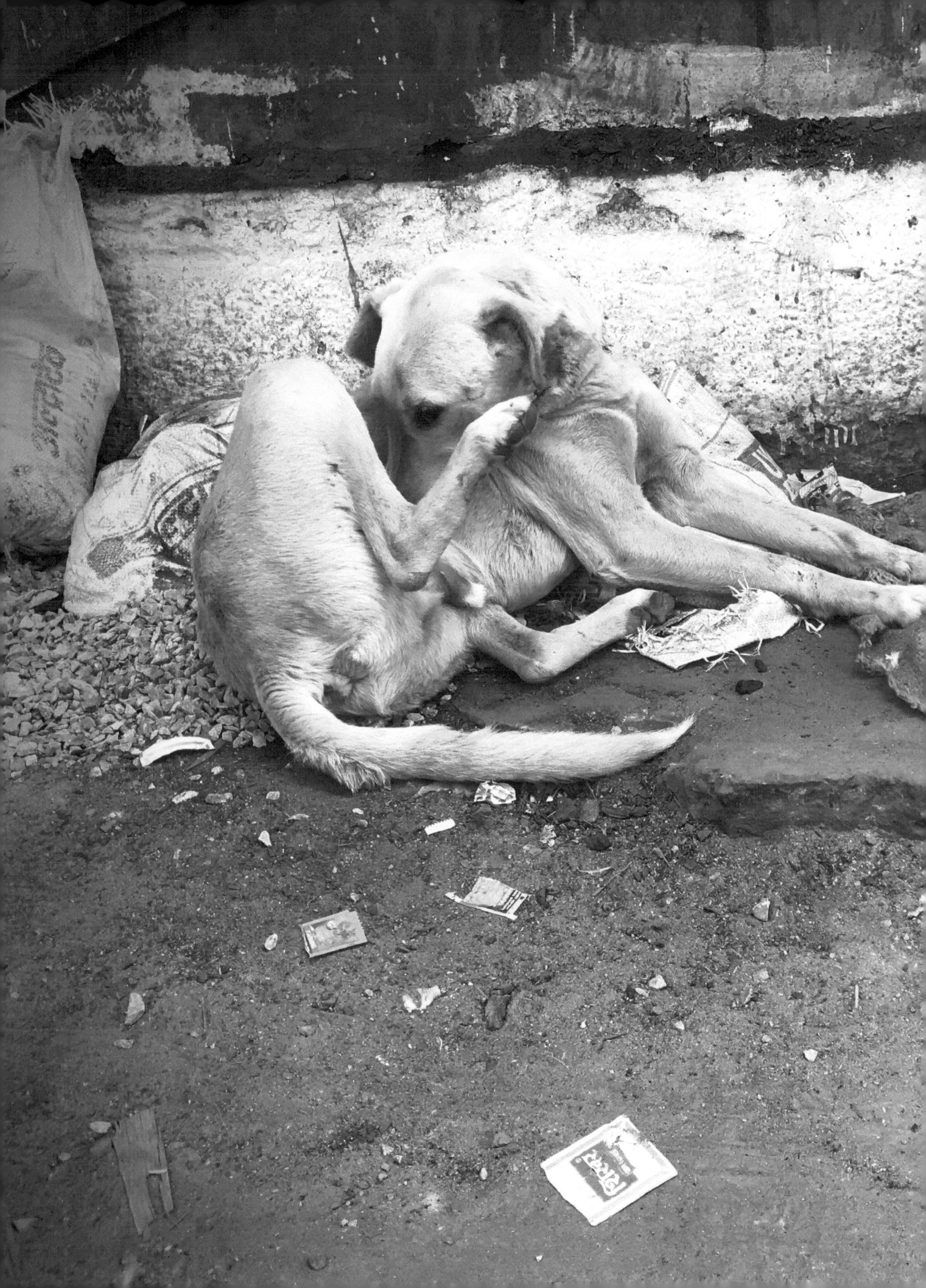

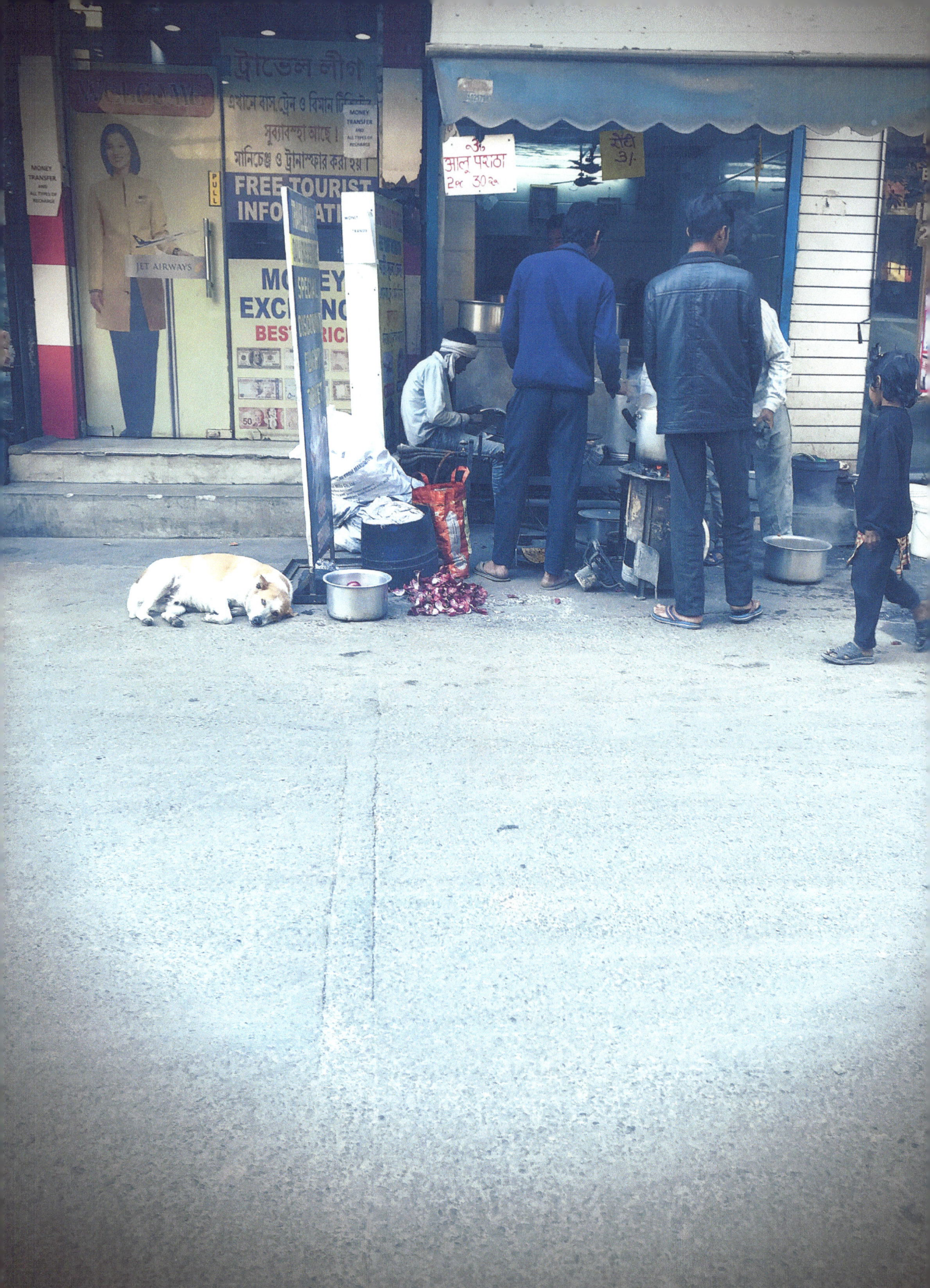

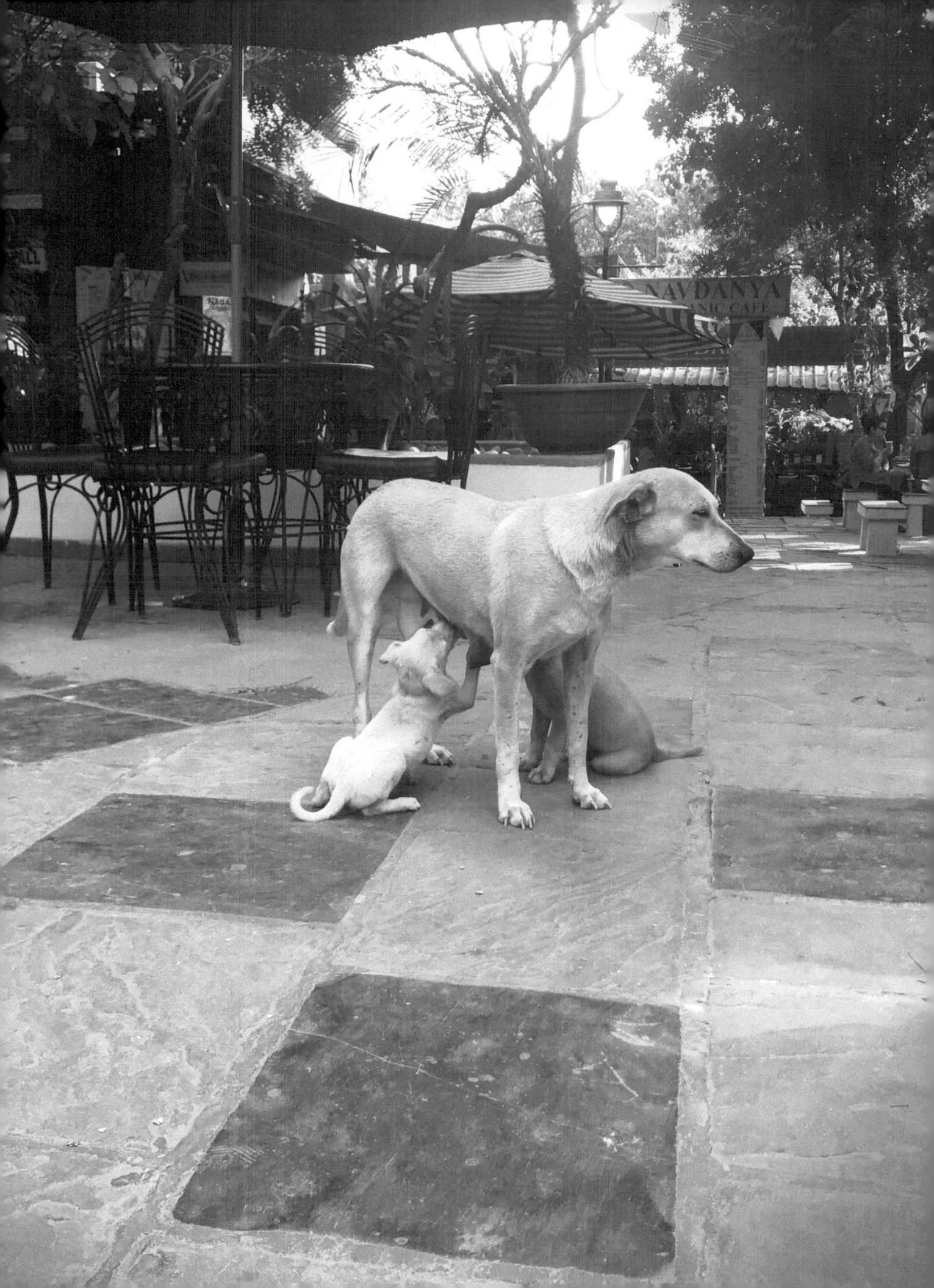

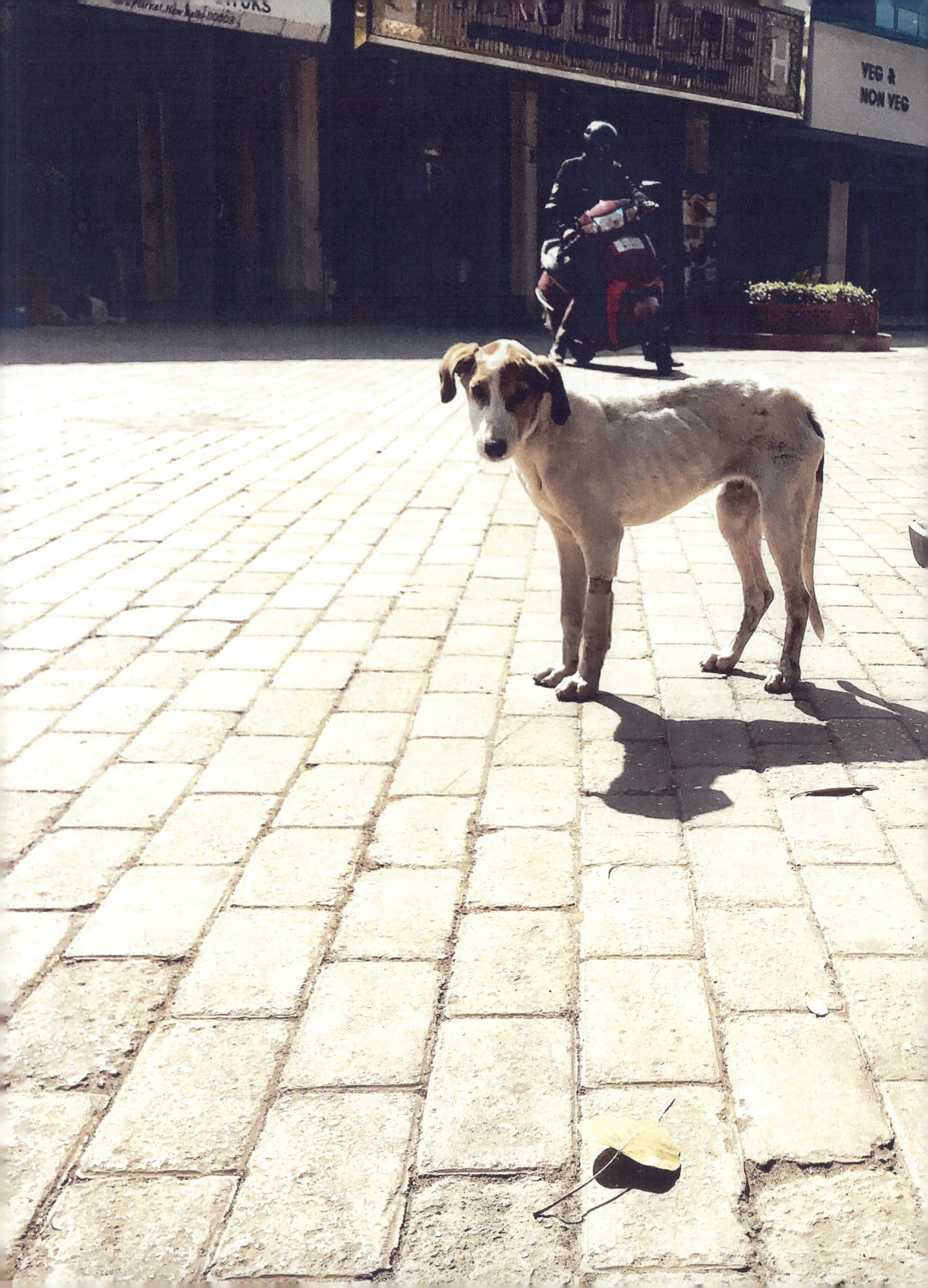

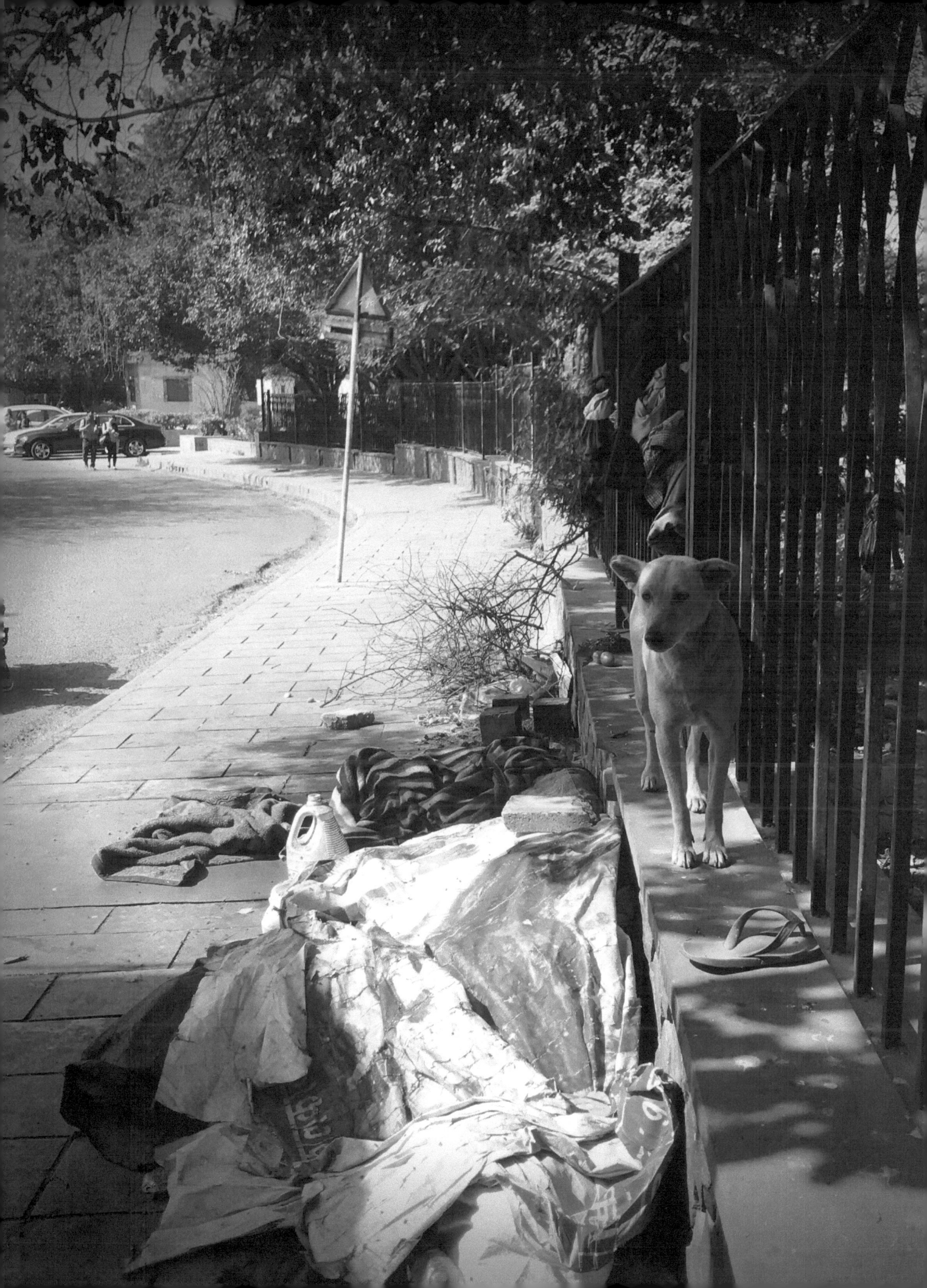

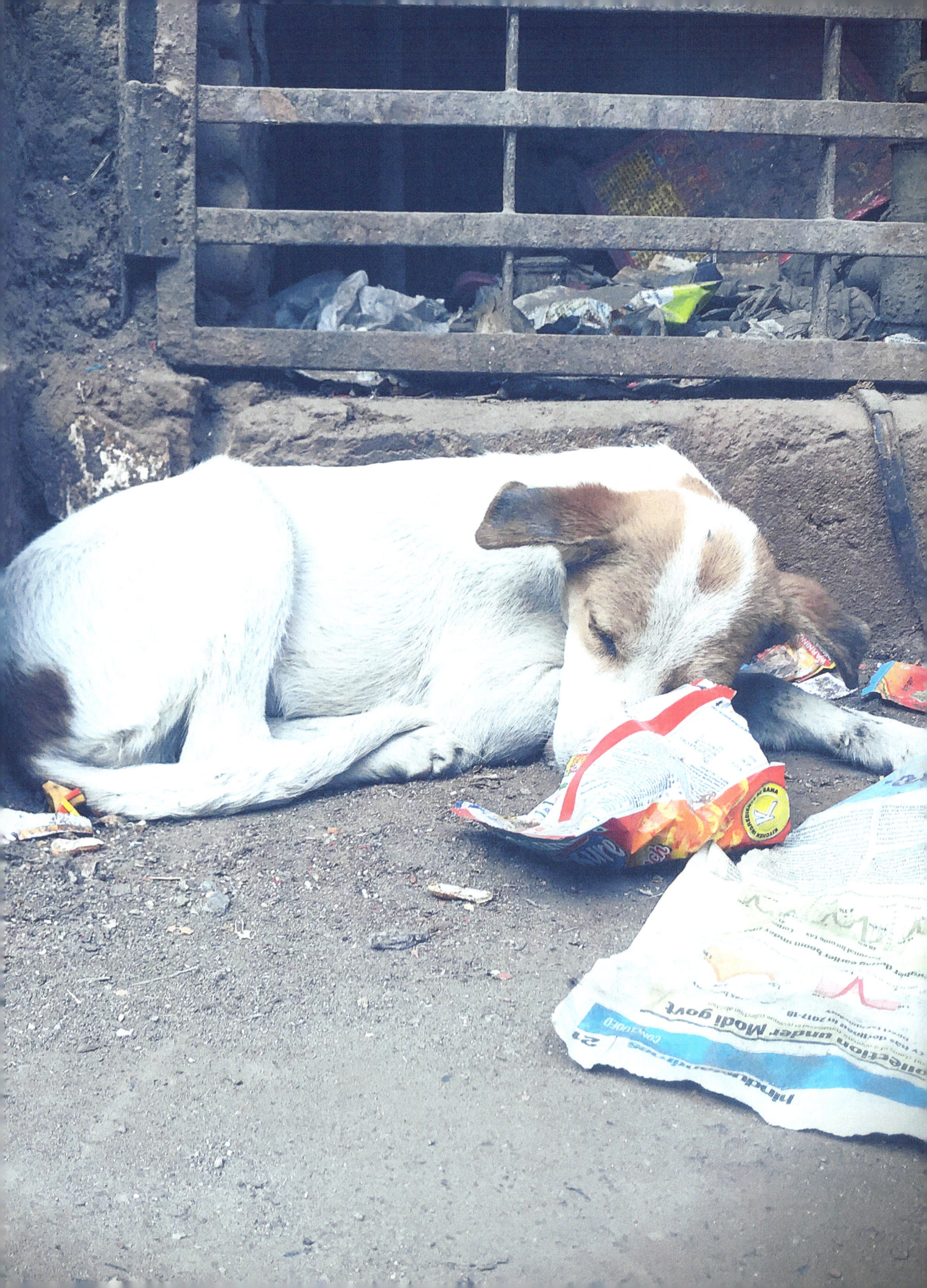

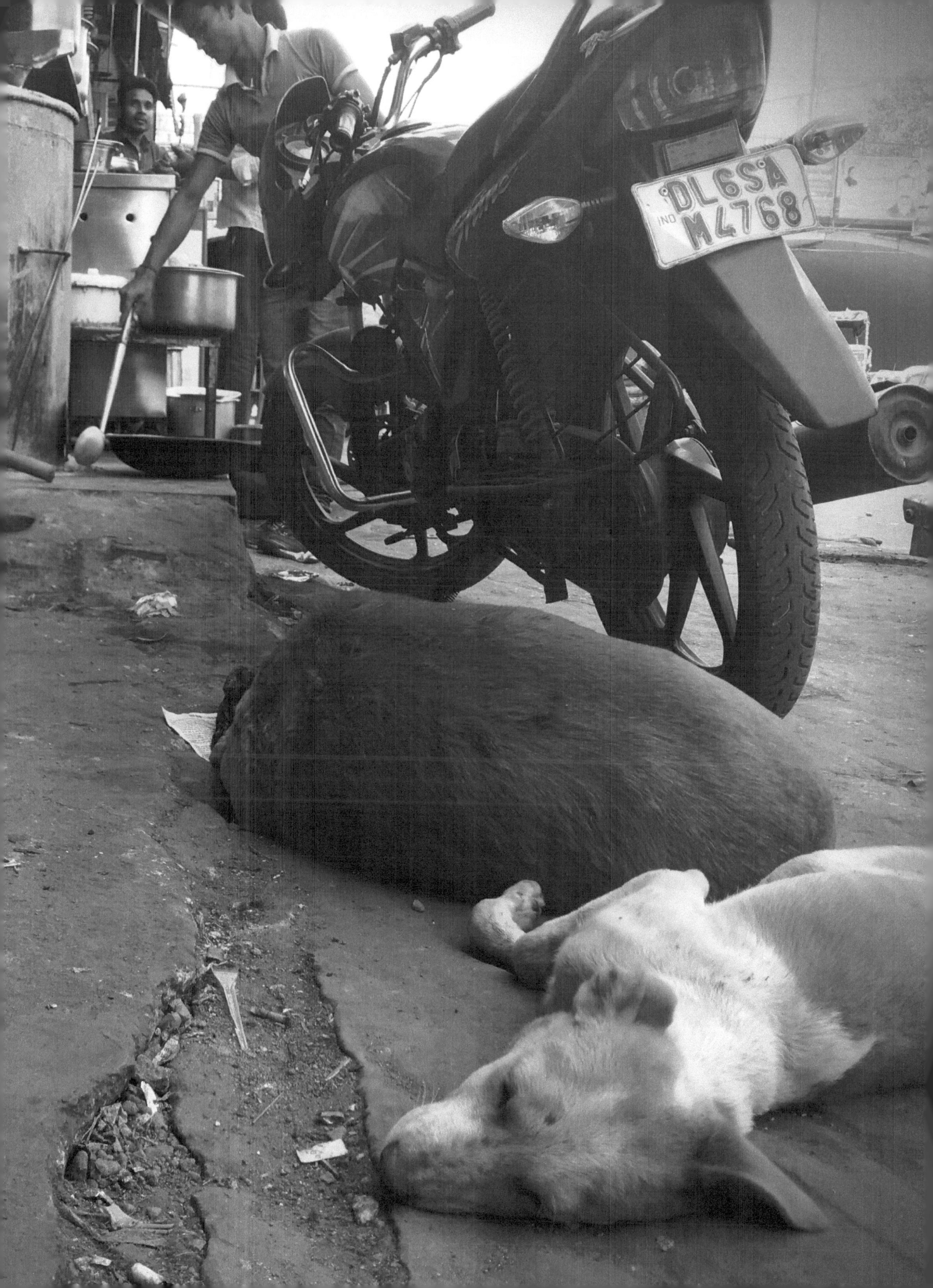

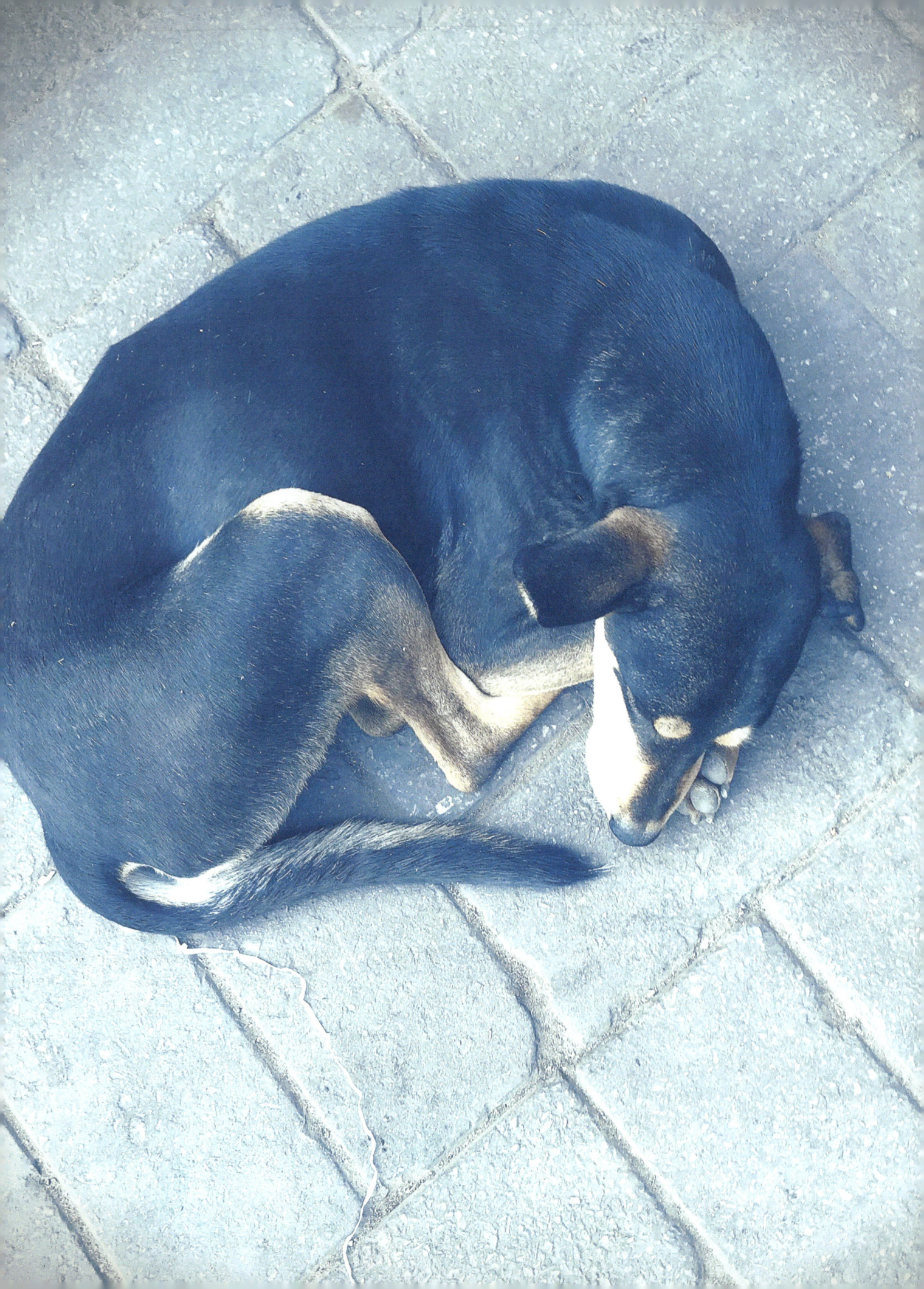

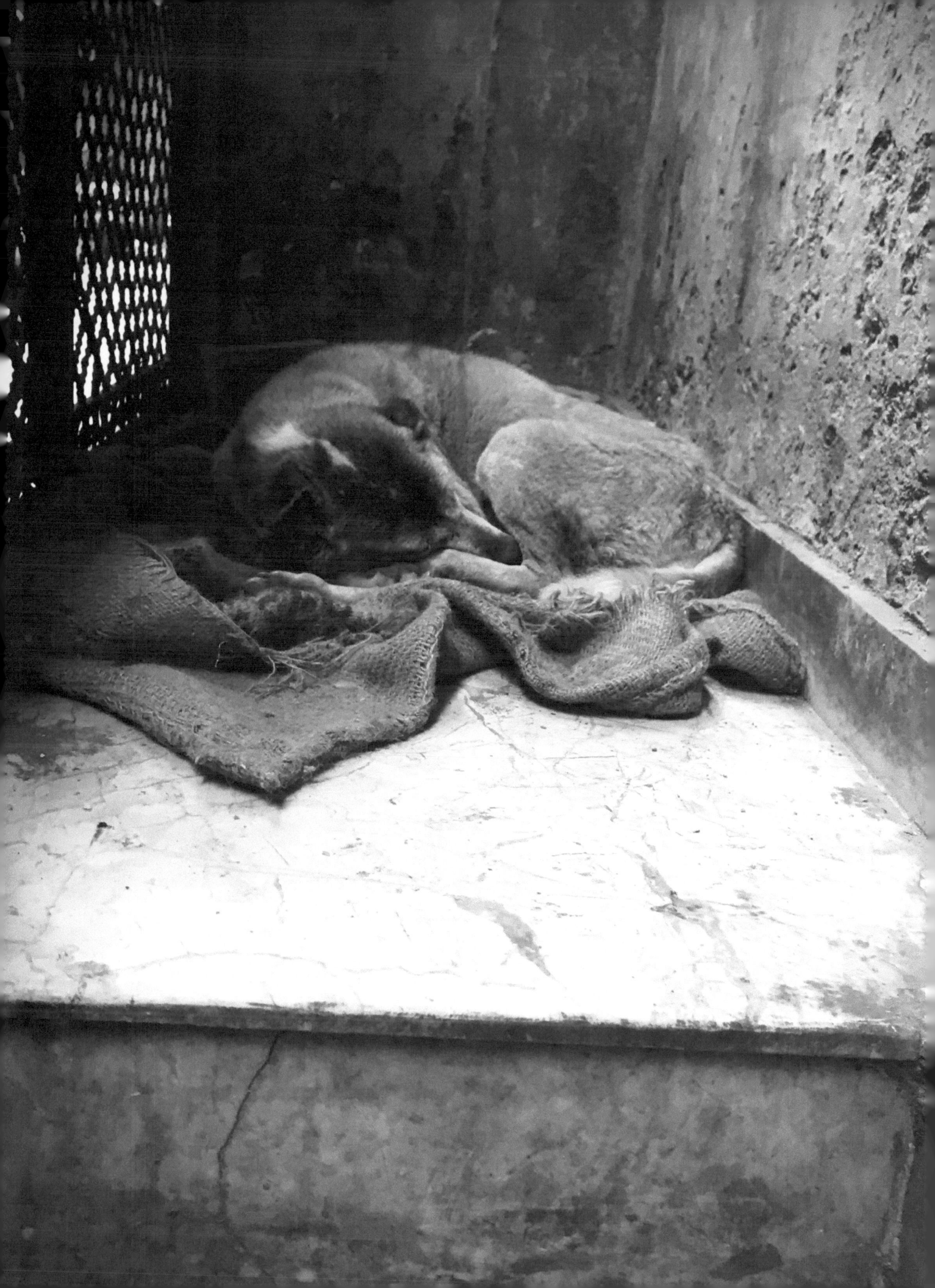

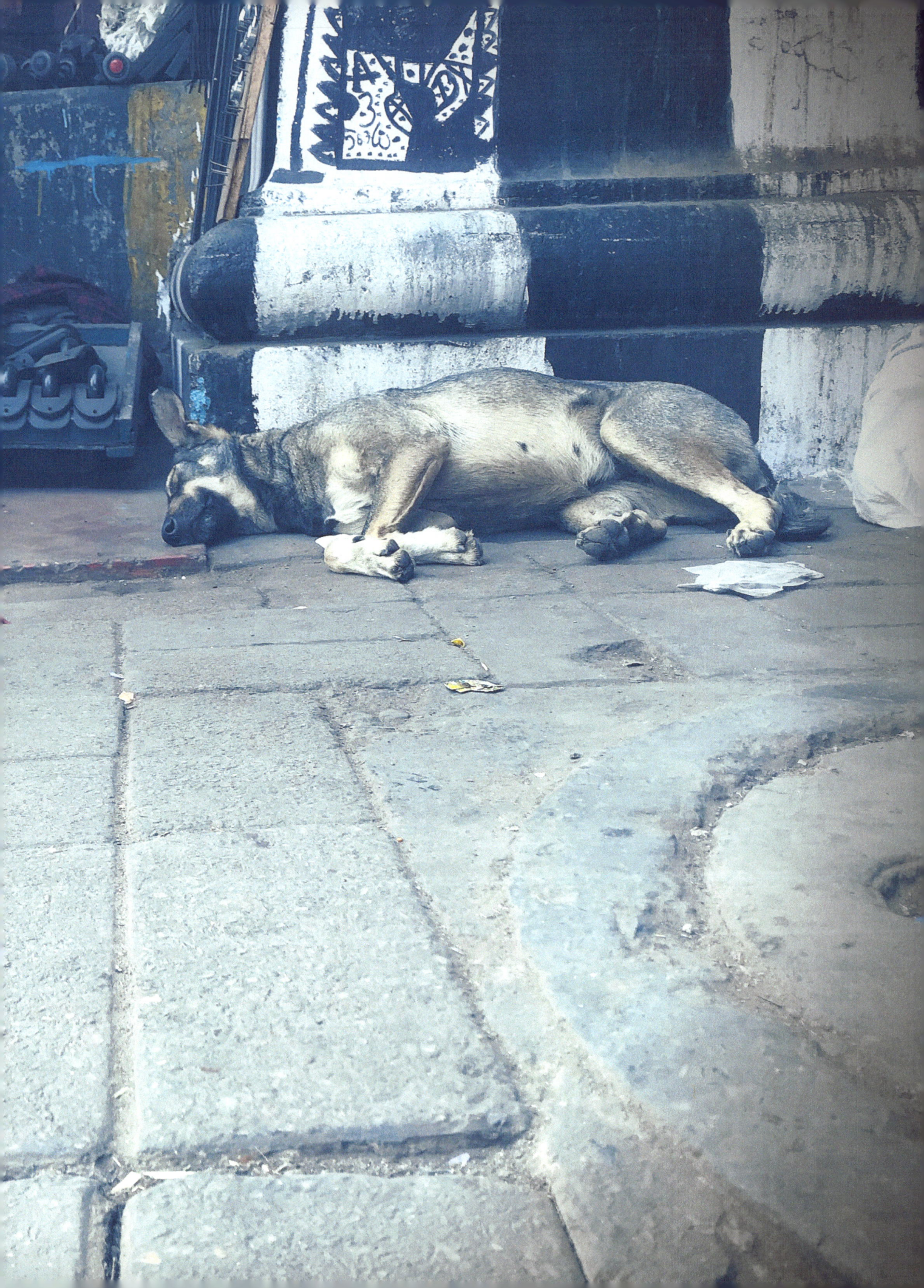

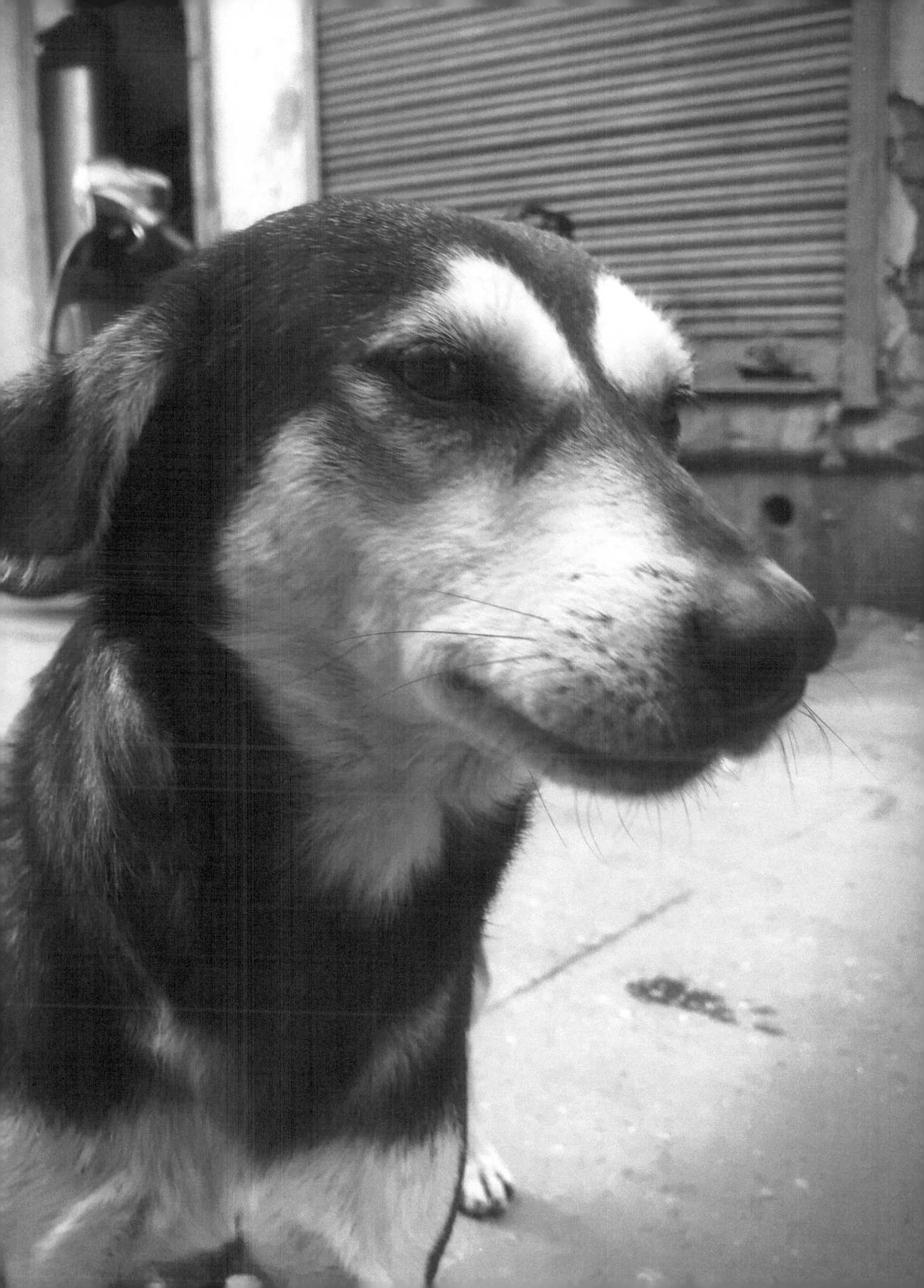

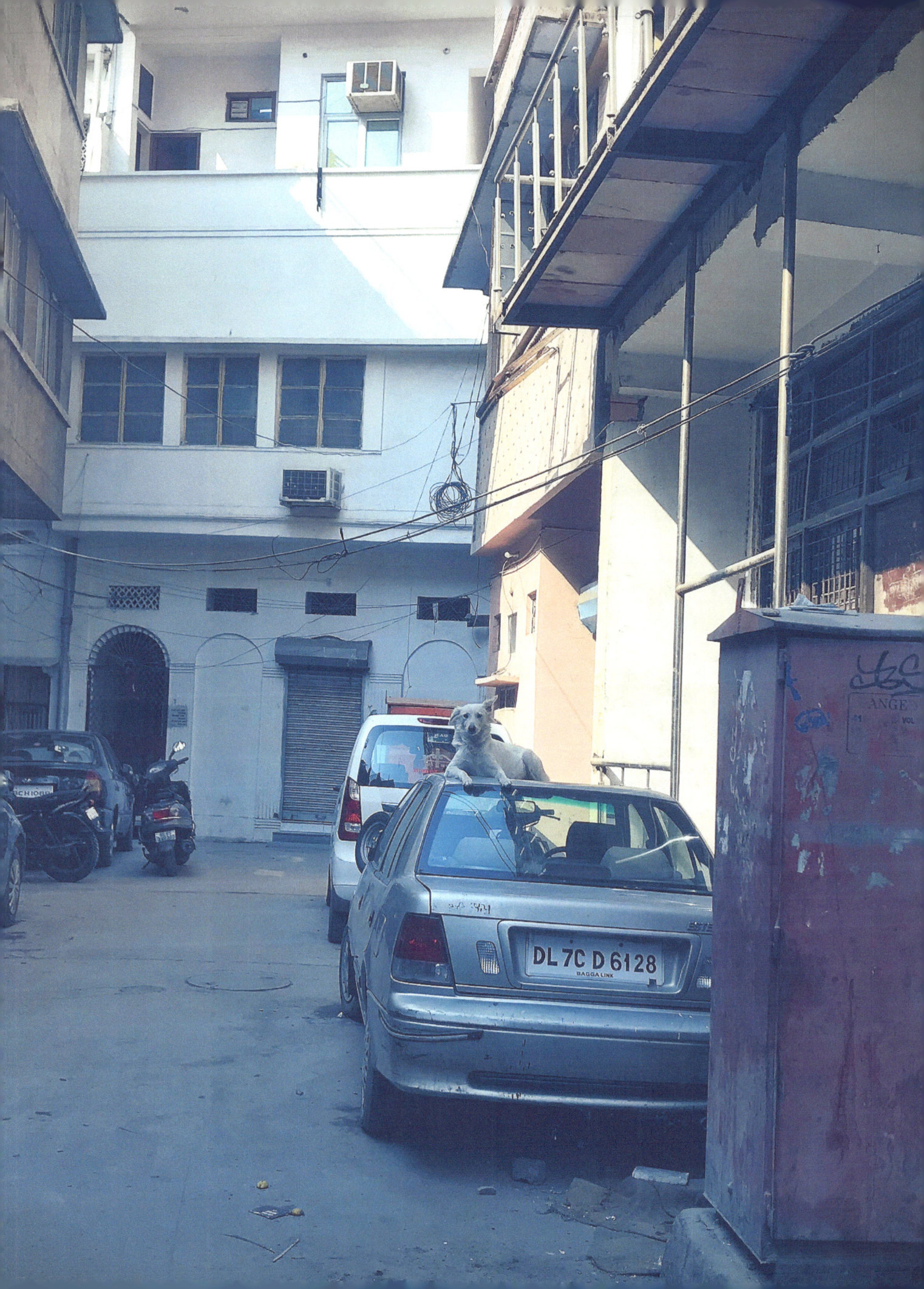

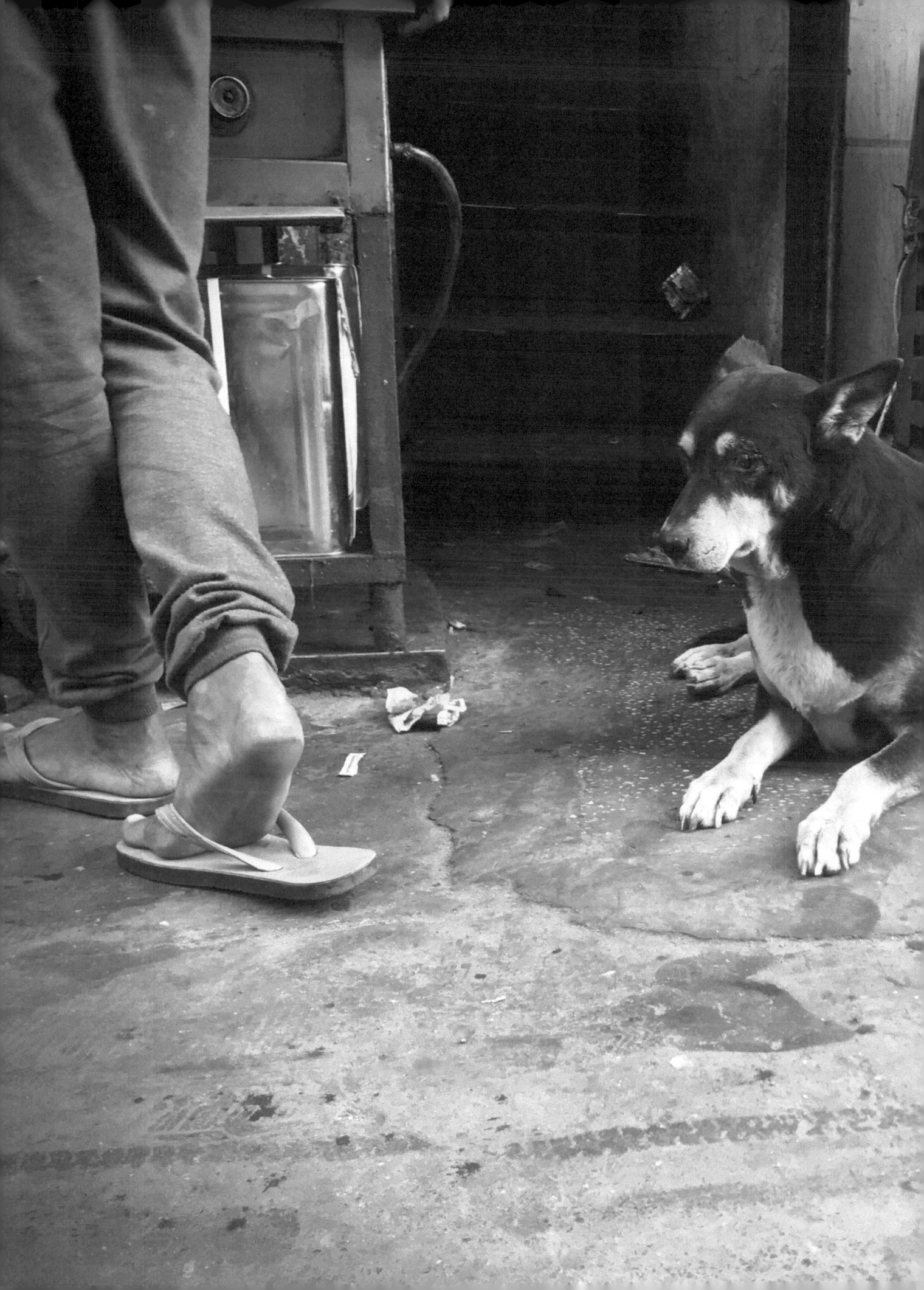

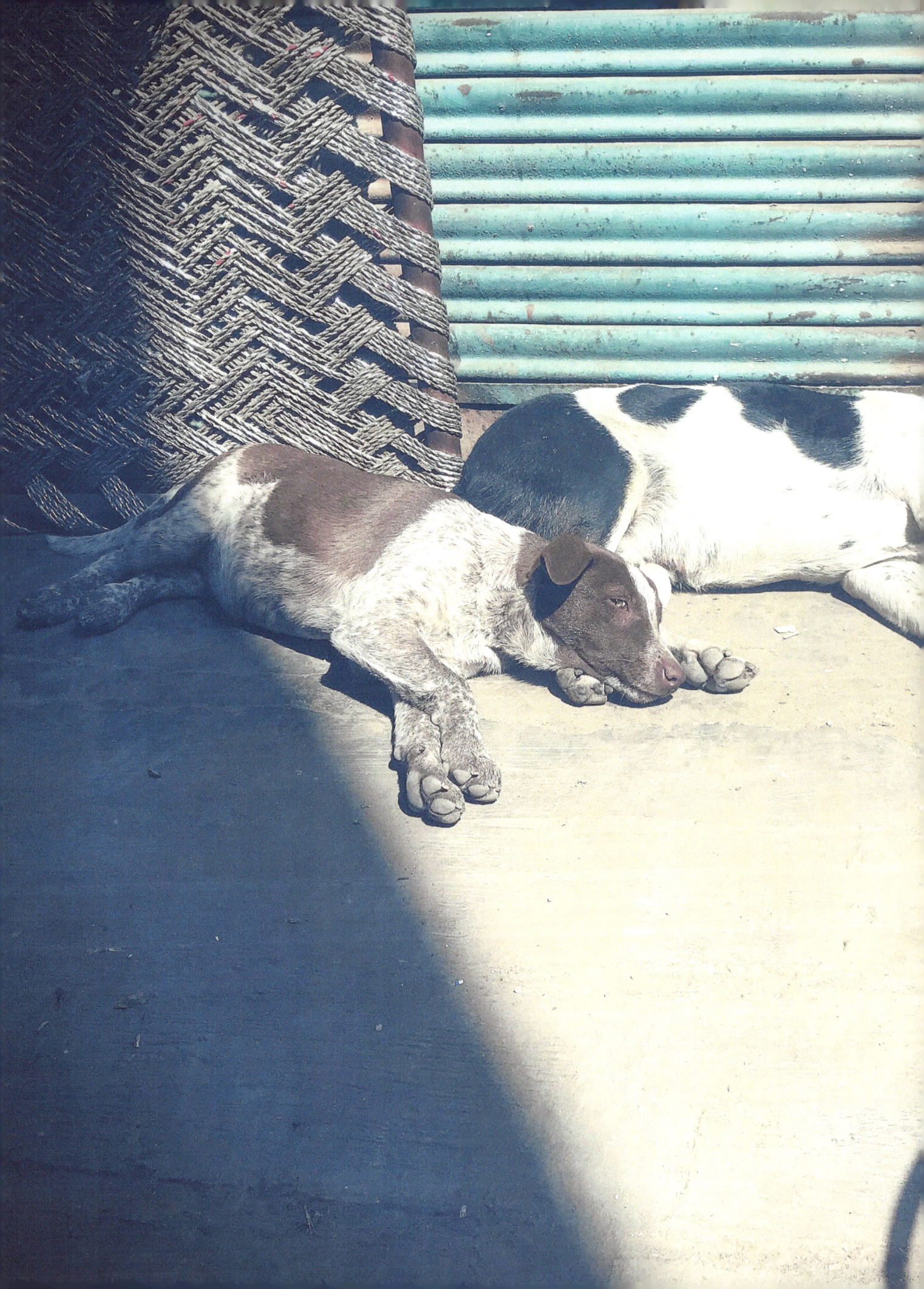

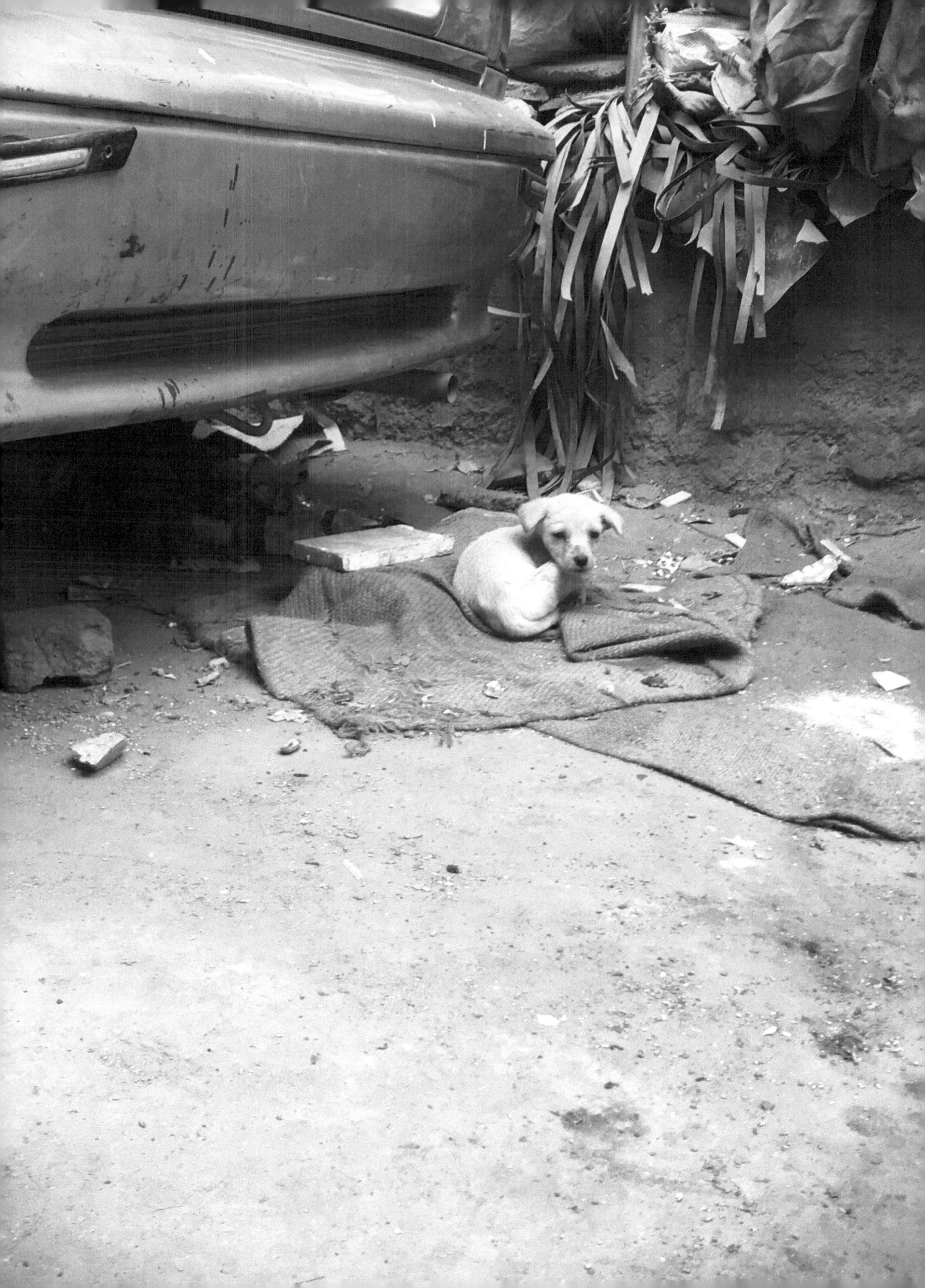

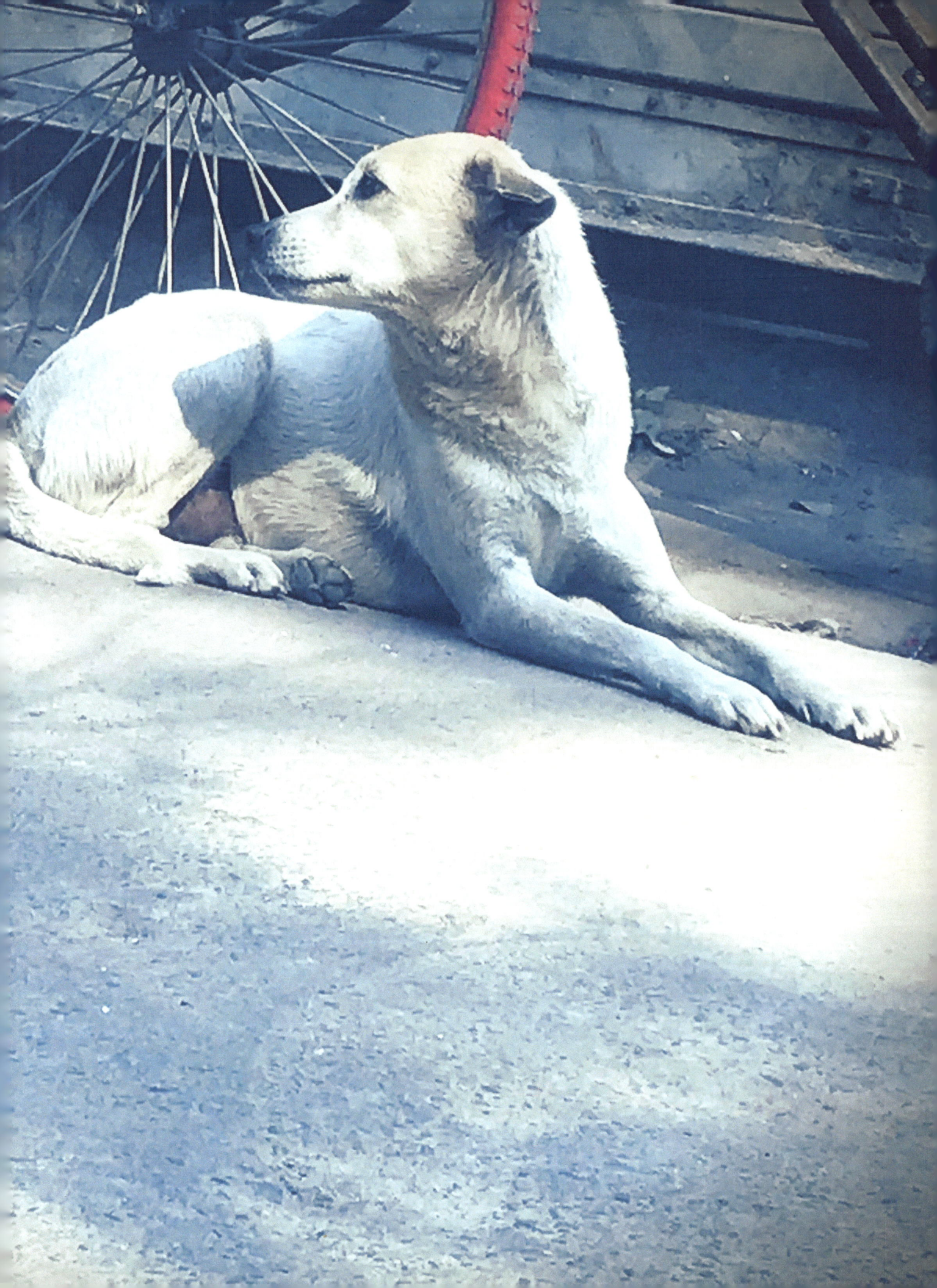

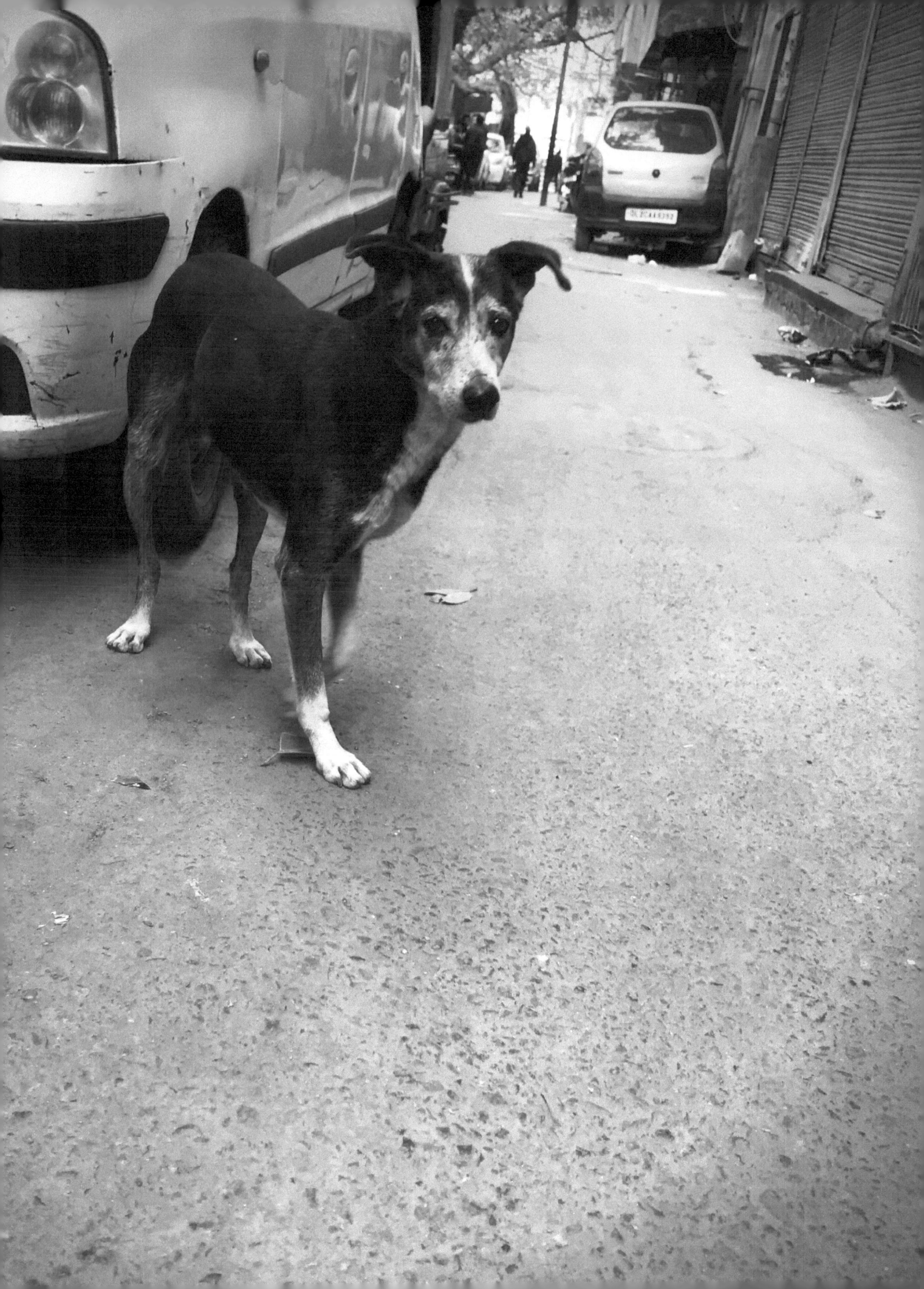

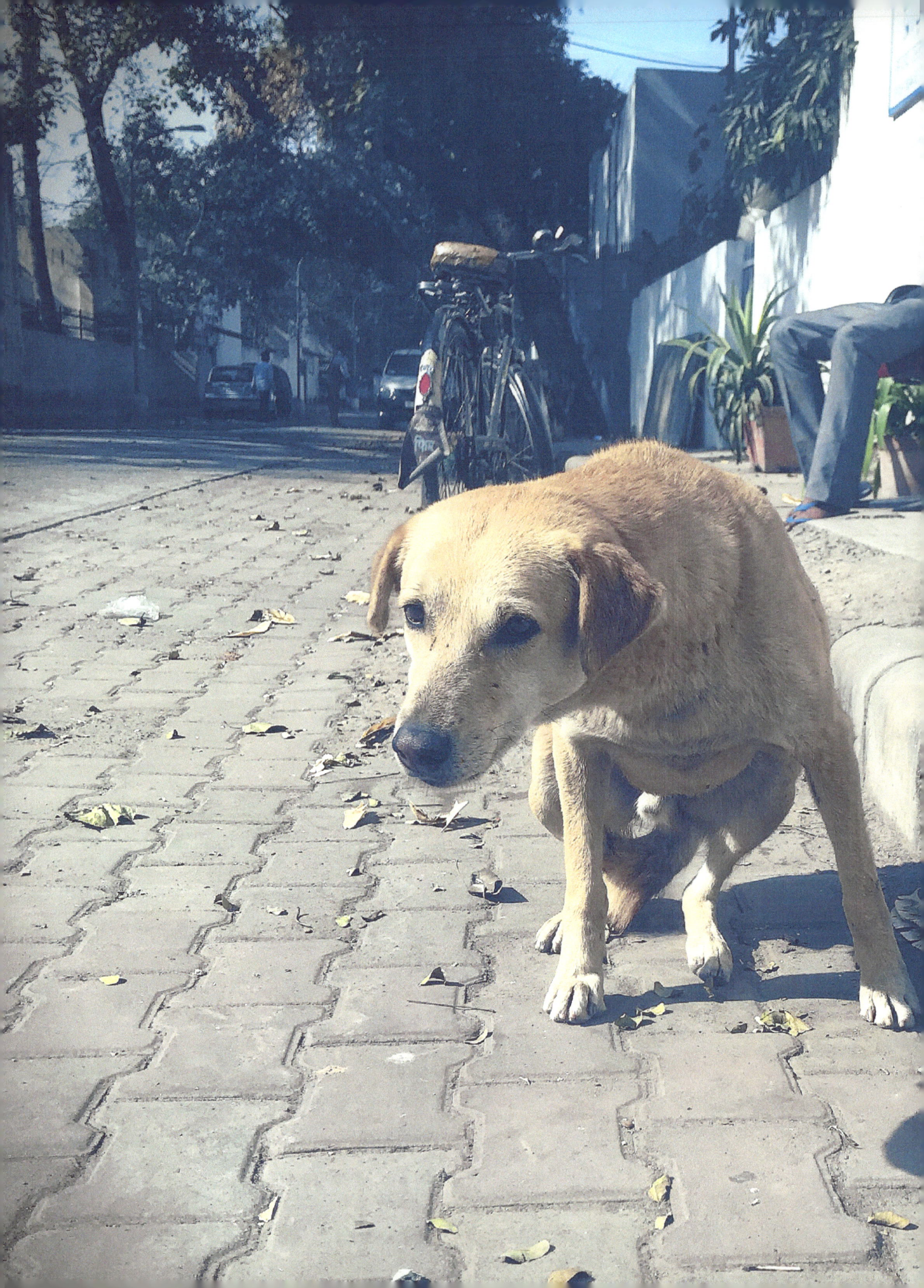

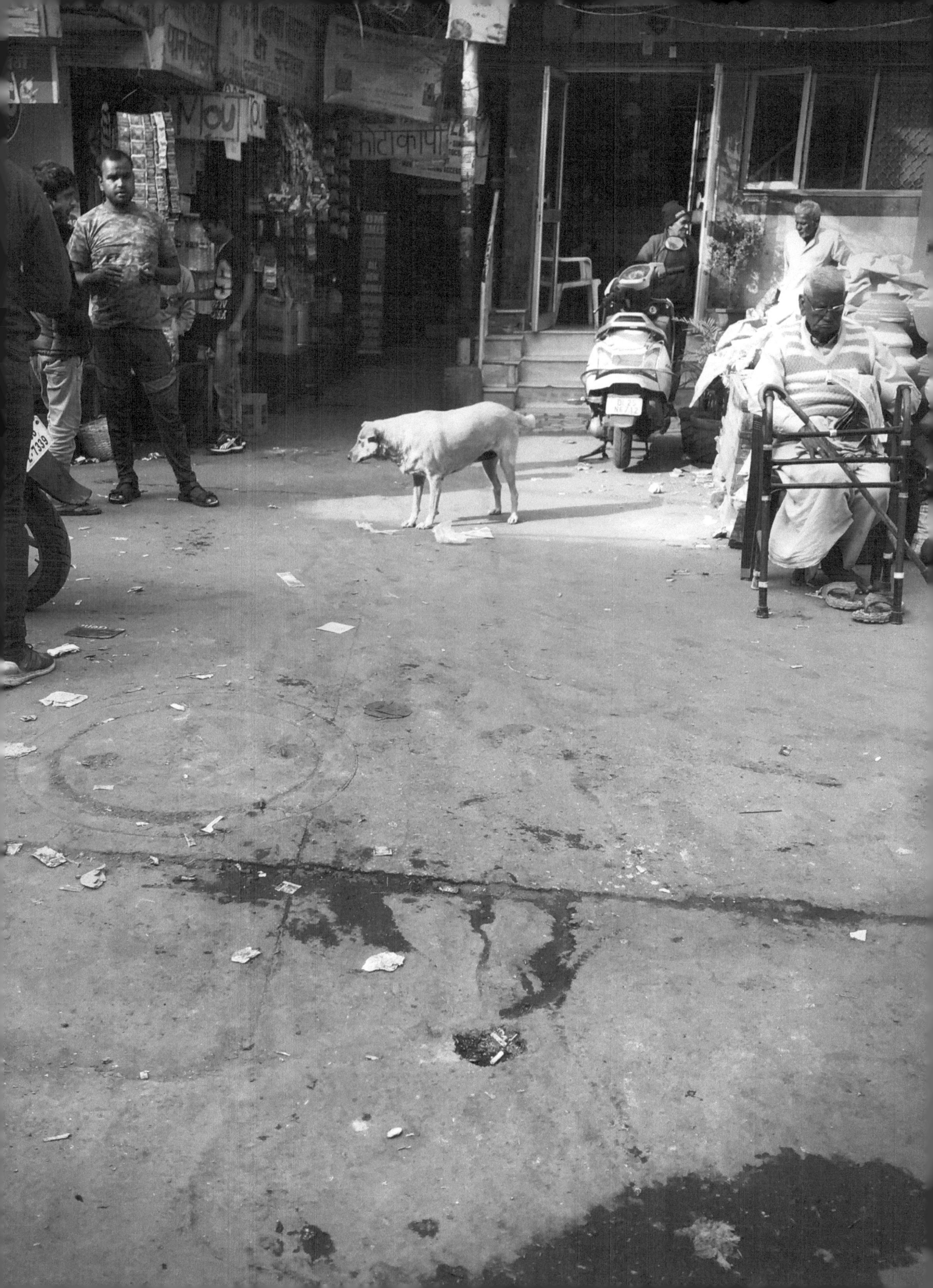

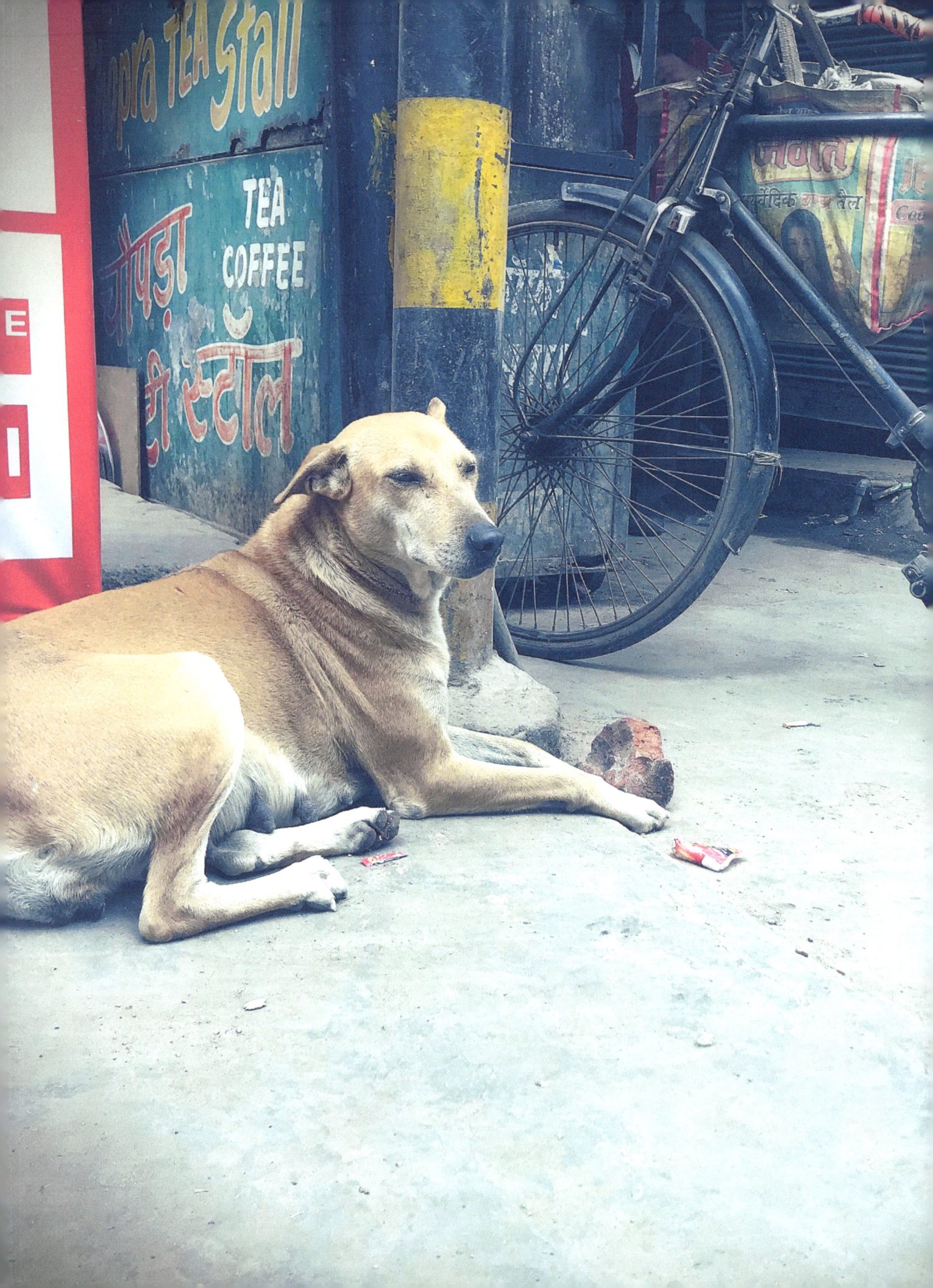

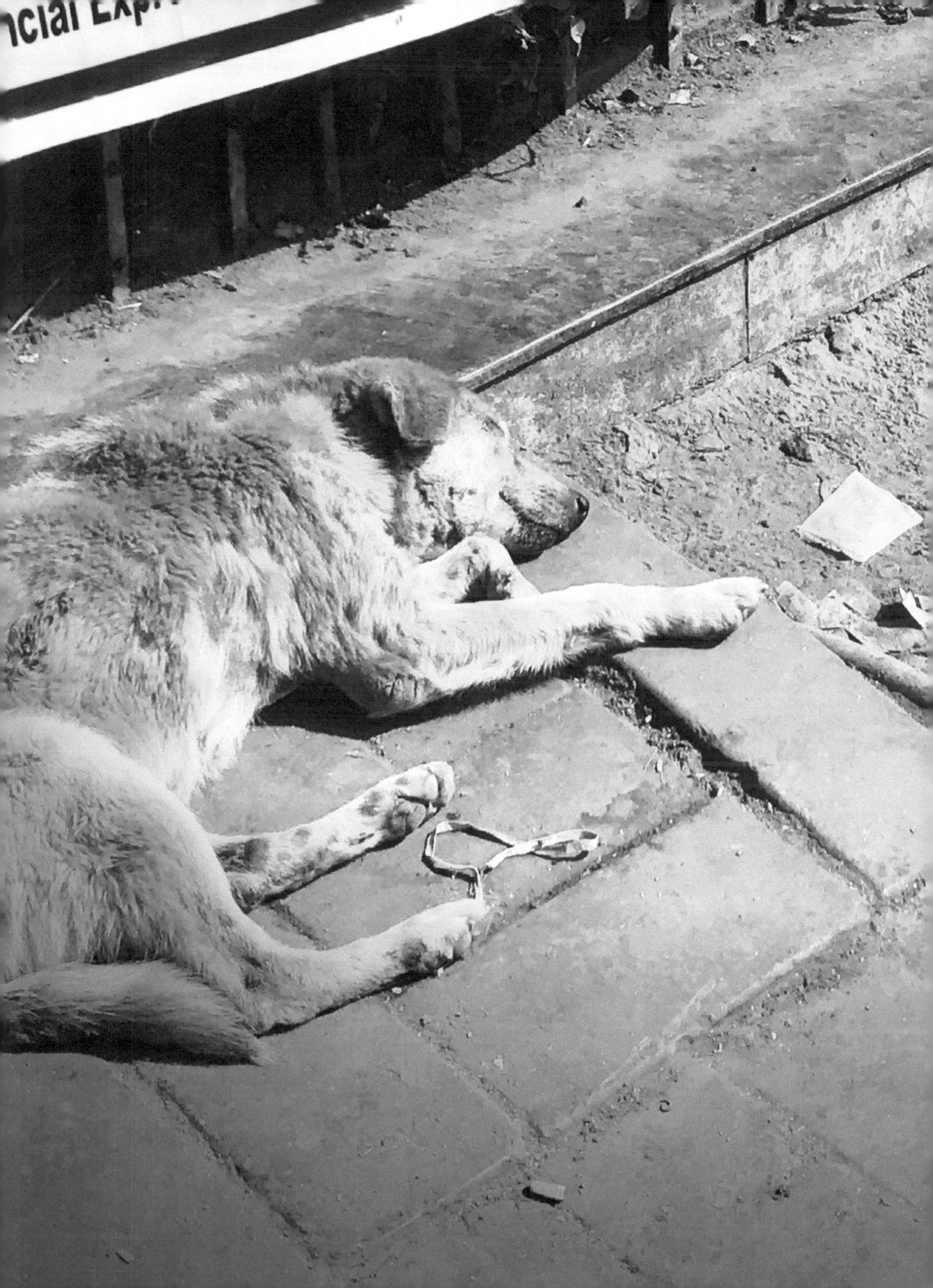

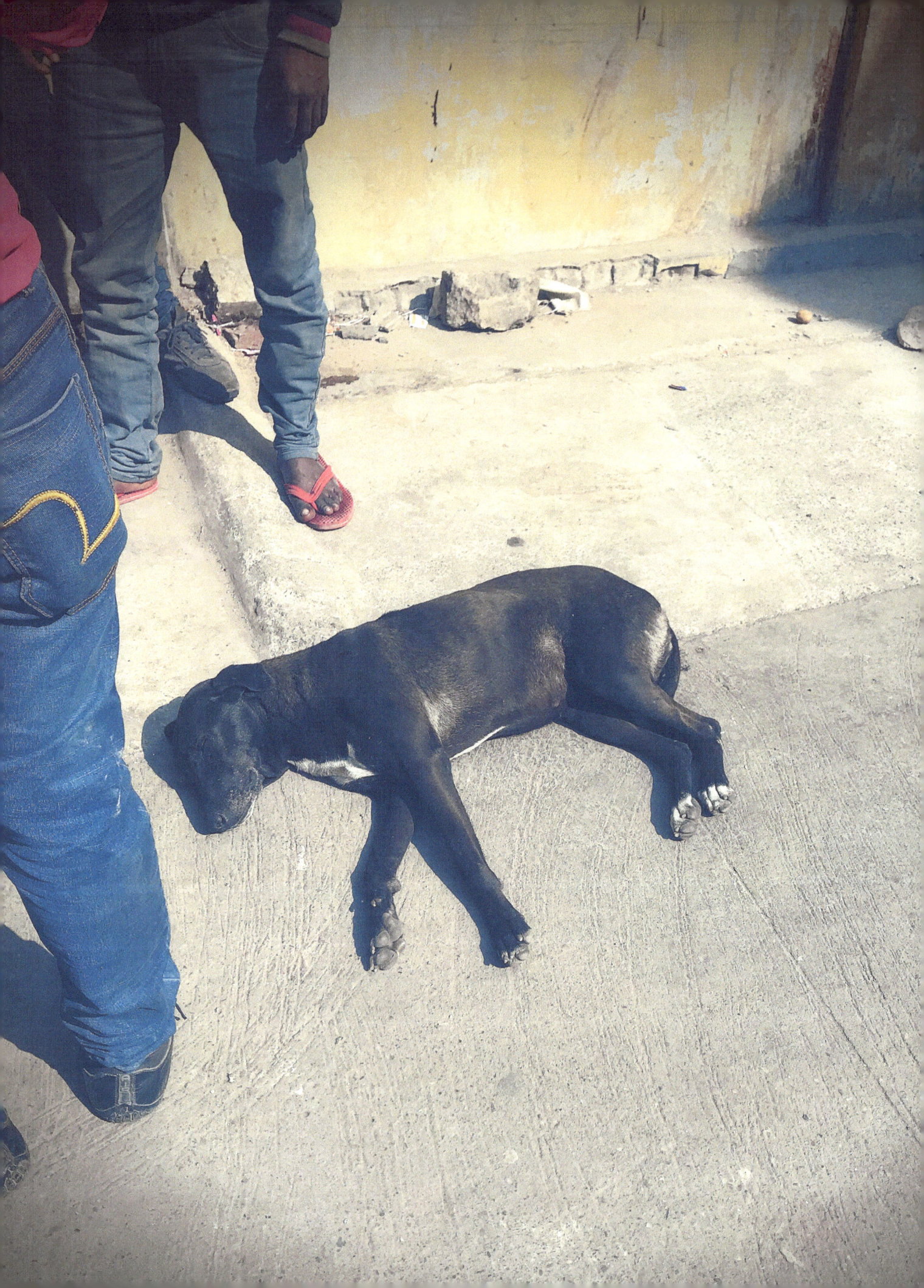

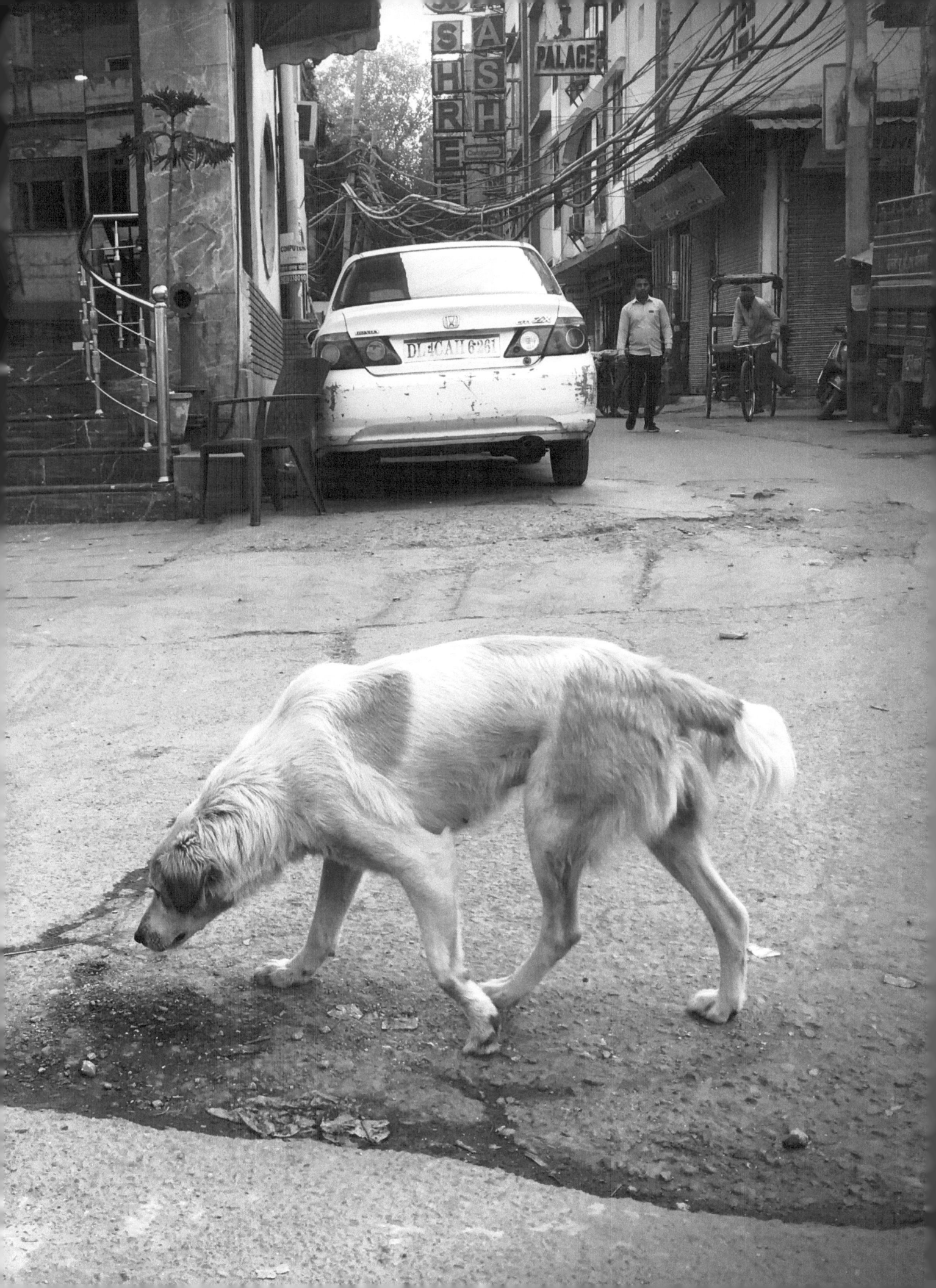

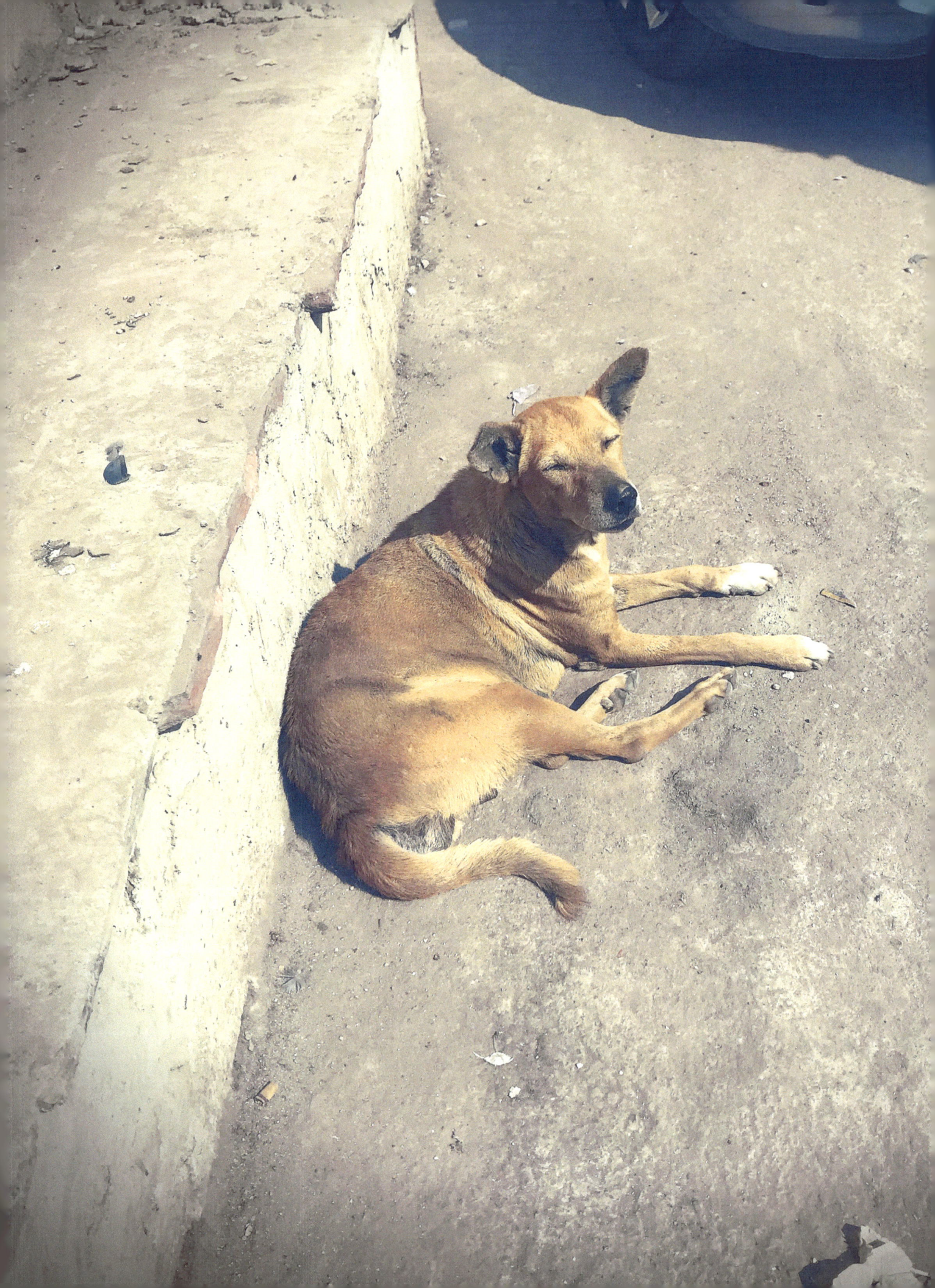

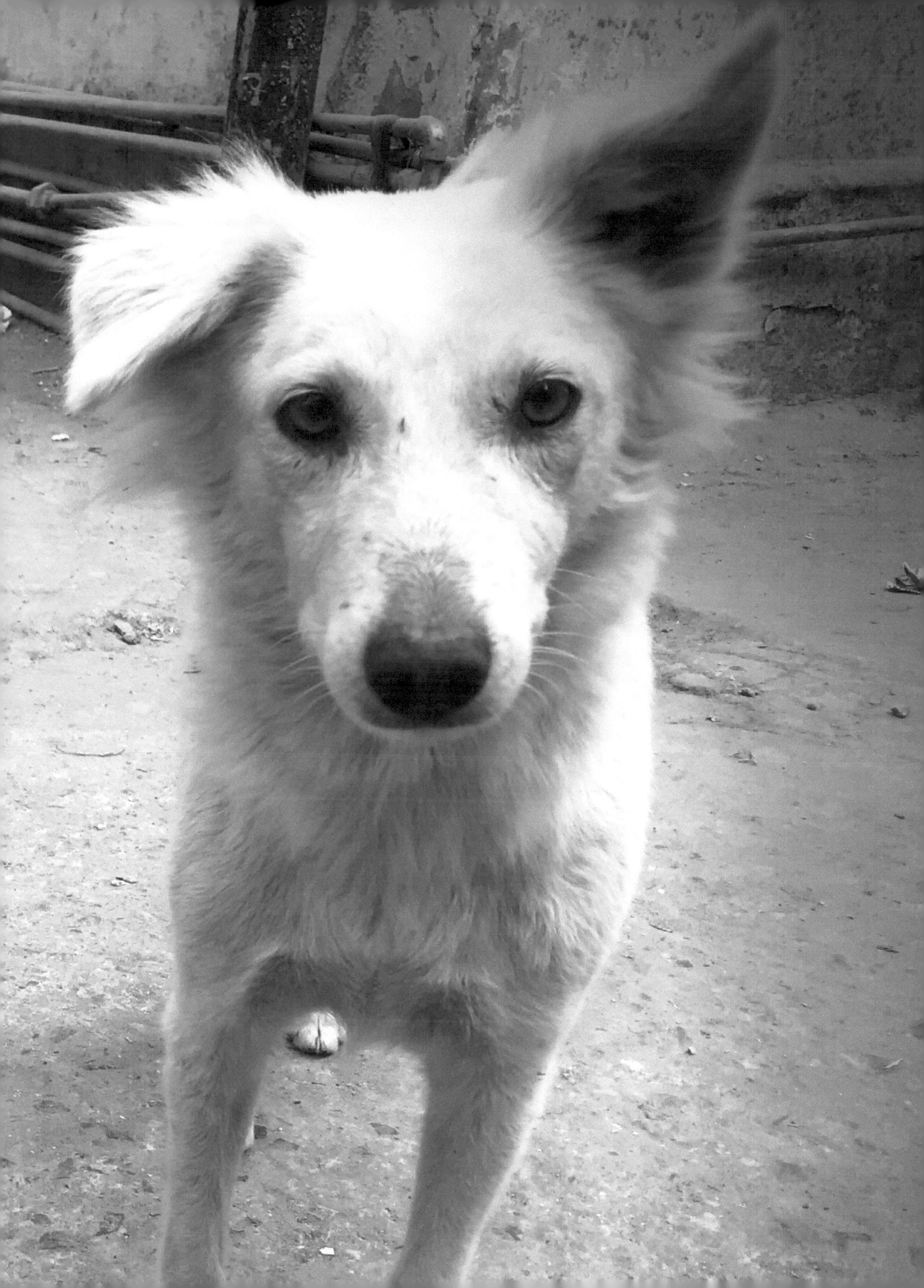

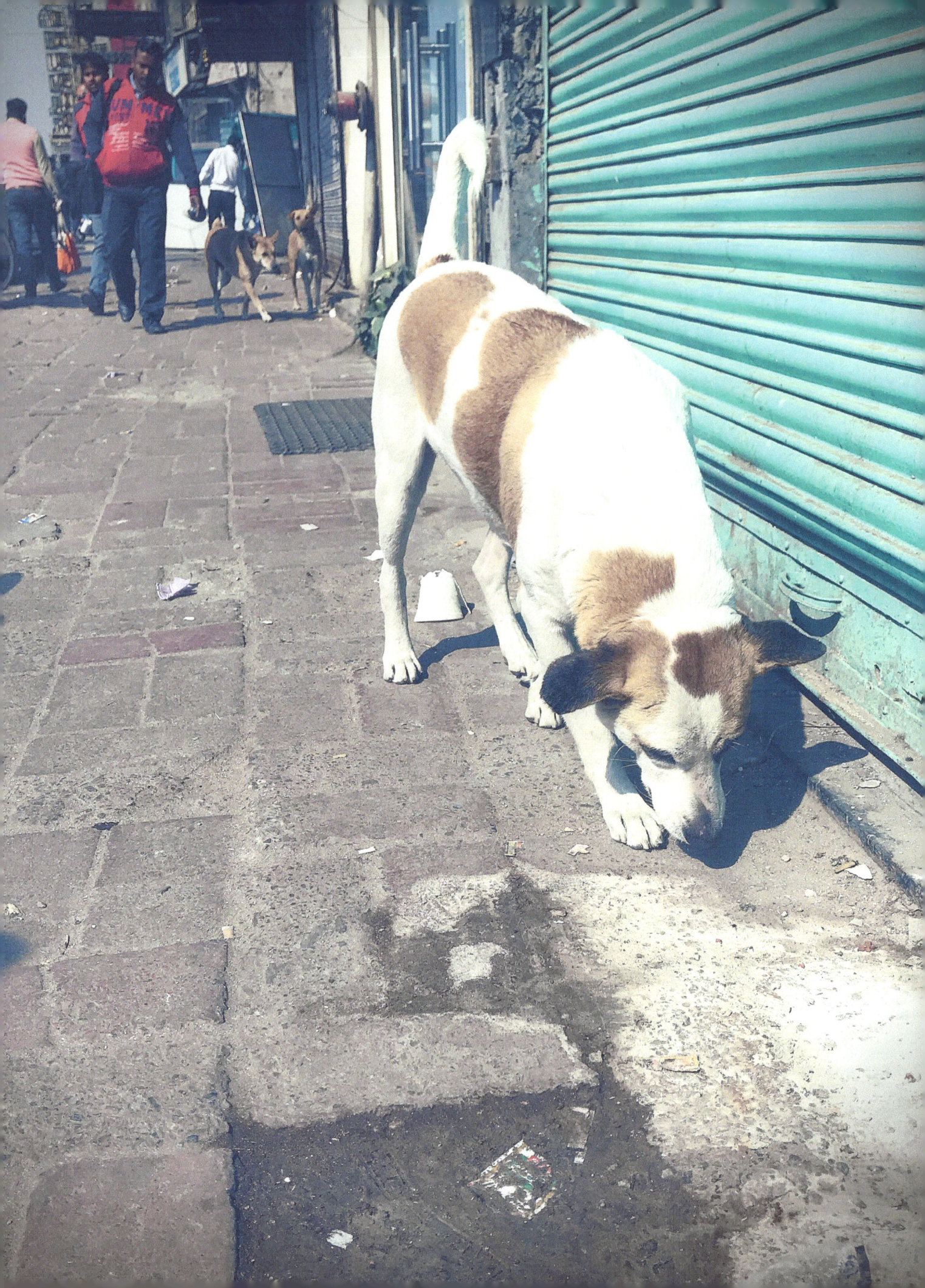

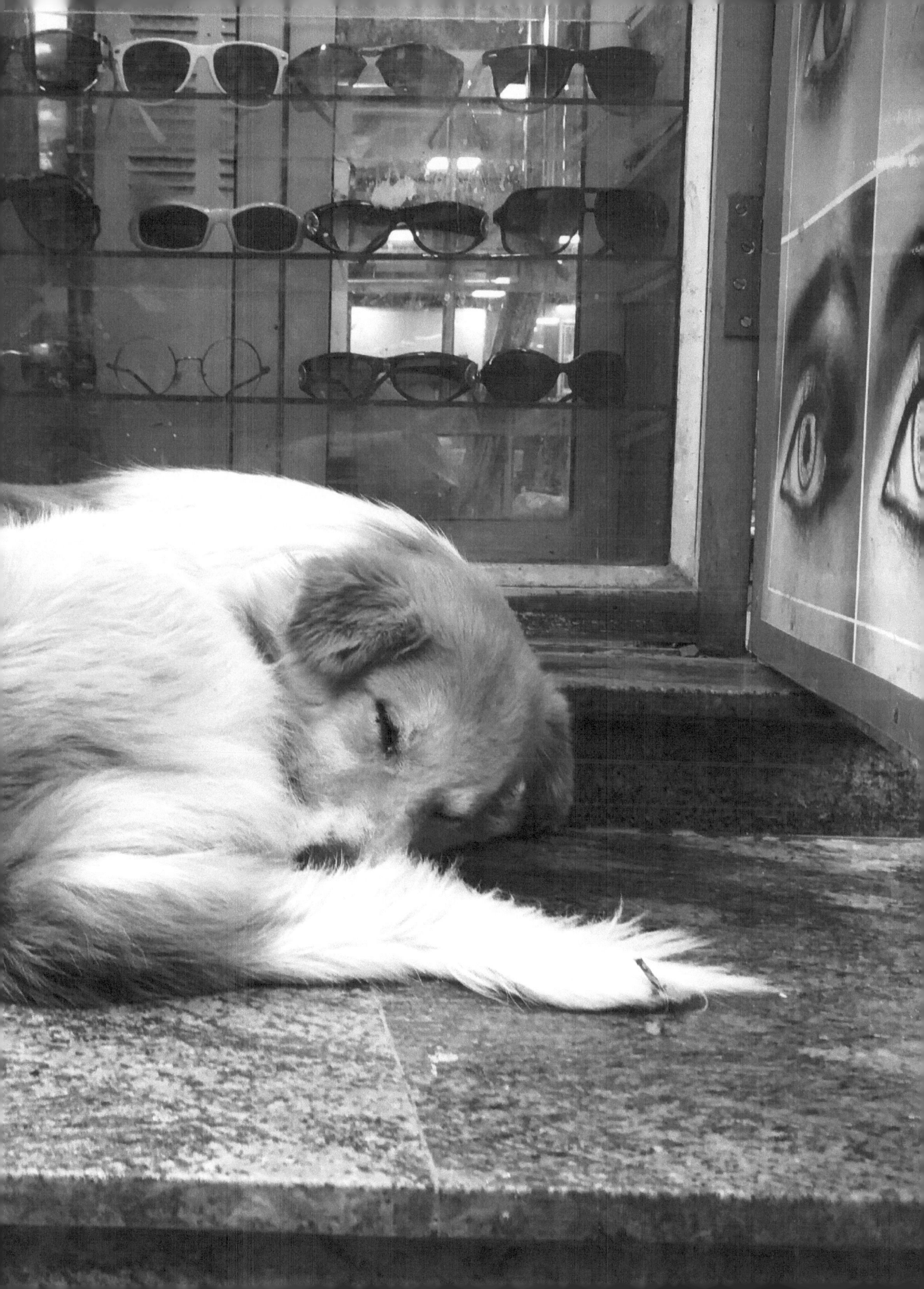

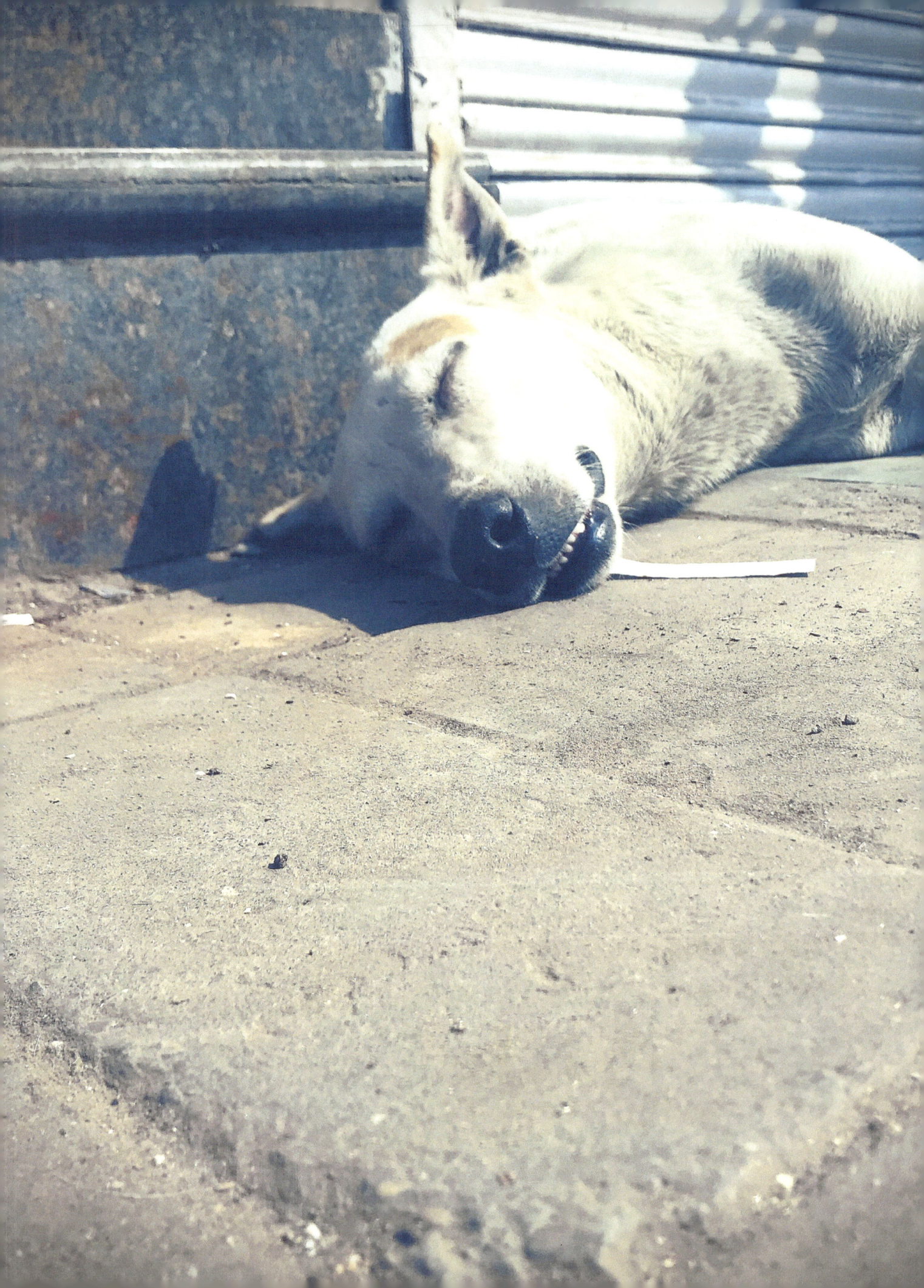

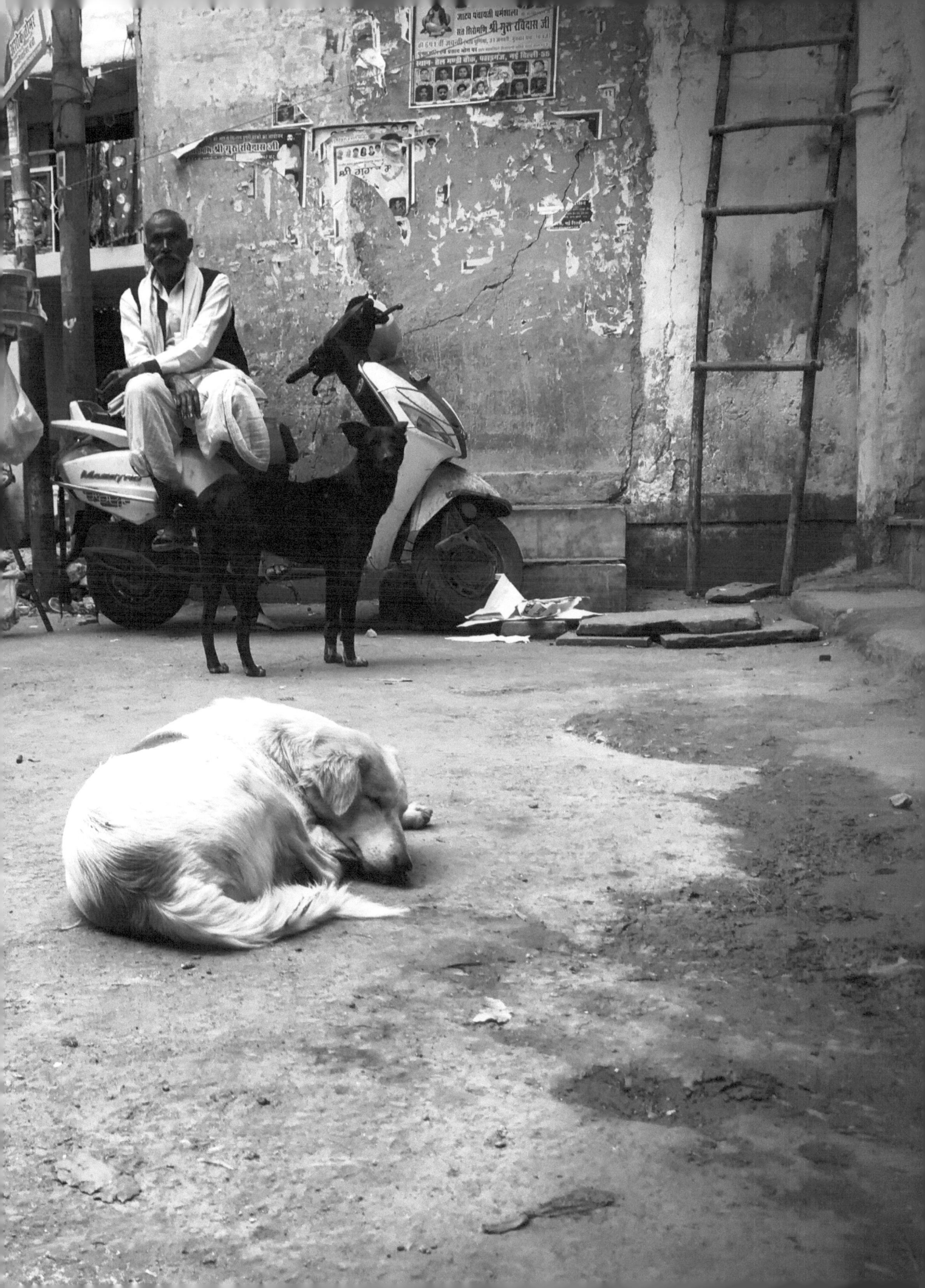

A PHOTOGRAPHIC JOURNEY OF
MUST LOVE METROPOLITAN MUTTS

MADE IN THE USA
NY, NY 10012
FEBUARY 2018

www.ingramcontent.com/pod-product-compliance
Lightning Source LLC
Chambersburg PA
CBHW051213220526
45473CB00003B/1010